# The Real Estate Millionaire

# The Real Estate Millionaire

## How to Invest in Rental Markets and Make a Fortune

Boaz Gilad

Suzanne Gilad

**McGraw-Hill**

New York Chicago San Francisco Lisbon London
Madrid Mexico City Milan New Delhi San Juan
Seoul Singapore Sydney Toronto

Copyright © 2006 by Boaz Gilad and Suzanne Gilad. All rights reserved. Printed in the United States of America. Except as permitted under the United States Copyright Act of 1976, no part of this publication may be reproduced or distributed in any form or by any means, or stored in a data base or retrieval system, without the prior written permission of the publisher.

1 2 3 4 5 6 7 8 9 10   DOC/DOC   0 9 8 7 6 5

ISBN 0-07-146577-4

McGraw-Hill books are available at special quantity discounts to use as premiums and sales promotions, or for use in corporate training programs. For more information, please write to the Director of Special Sales, Professional Publishing, McGraw-Hill, Two Penn Plaza, New York, NY 10121-2298. Or contact your local bookstore.

 This book is printed on recycled, acid-free paper containing a minimum of 50% recycled, de-inked fiber.

Library of Congress Cataloging-in-Publication Data
Gilad, Boaz.
  The real estate millionaire : how to invest in rental markets and make a fortune / Boaz Gilad and Suzanne Gilad.— 1st ed.
    p. cm.
  Includes index.
  ISBN 0-07-146577-4 (alk. paper)
 1.  Real estate investment—United States. 2.  Real property—Purchasing—United States.
3.  Rental housing—United States.  I. Gilad, Suzanne. II. Title.
  HD255.G54  2006
  332.63'243—dc22

                                                              2005025272

*To Our Parents*
*With Love*

# Acknowledgments

We would like to thank the original BST Real Estate members, especially Shmuel Gilad and Tom McNiff.

Further gratitude goes to Stretch Merced, Yossi Ariel, Michael Larsen and Elizabeth Pomada (agents extraordinaire), and Landmark Education.

A special thank you to Laura Jorstad, who has provided support throughout. Also to Andrew Gitzy, whose wonderful input has helped shape our ideas.

# Contents

# Contents

# Contents

# Introduction
## Real Estate and
## Why We Love It

*There are two kinds of people, separated by a chasm: Those who have real estate, and those who don't.*

*—Anonymous*

*Lucy: I never get what I really want for Christmas.*
*Charlie Brown: What's that?*
*Lucy: Real estate.*

*—The Charlie Brown Christmas Special*

Let's not dance around. I know why you're here. You want to make some money. If possible, a lot of money. Everyone is looking for a route to financial independence and freedom from the daily grind.

Real estate is, and always has been, the cornerstone of wealth. Did you know that the word *real* in real estate doesn't come from its material nature, but instead from the French and Spanish word for "royal"? In ancient times, kings raised armies, nations fell, and new ones were born, all in the name of real estate. It still happens today. And why? Fundamentally, land is *the* basic human need: We need food, water, and shelter. All three of these things come from the land we live on. Our territory, if you will.

Makes it all sound very grand, doesn't it? Not anymore. For centuries, real estate belonged only to the affluent and powerful, but today every Tom, Dick, and Harriet can get rich thanks to real estate investment.

Maybe you've only begun to think about real estate investment. Maybe you've already read a few books on the subject and are wondering why you still need help understanding what *escrow* is. Or maybe you're looking for that special book that will show how to become the property mogul you always thought you could be! In any case, you've come to the right place. *The Real Estate Millionaire* lets everyone in on the ancient secret of property ownership as the foundation of extreme wealth.

## So Who Am I?

If three years ago anyone told me that I would be a real estate mogul, I probably would have laughed. Loudly. I grew up in a household that did not place importance on making megabucks. Quite the opposite; we equated wealth with corruption.

I fell into real estate investment by pure chance. This livelihood grew out of a desire to be financially independent and pursue whatever I wanted to—that is, I wanted enough money to fund my dreams. My first career choice was acting. My love for the arts was so strong that in my teens I moved away from home to attend acting school. Then, as a young adult, I moved to New York City to study philosophy and acting. Two big money-makers, right? (*Not!*) Like anyone else, of course, I needed to pay the bills. True to the stereotype, I worked as a waiter for a while, but I knew I wanted to find a way to make more money.

I investigated alternative sources of income, and real estate investment caught my eye. But how could I make that work? I didn't have any money. I didn't have any experience or connections. What *did* I have? Well, my time and my commitment. With these on my side, then, I was able to convince several investors to take a risk on me and supply me with the money to purchase my first property. (This, amazingly, was easy. You'll find out how to do it in Chapter 5.) So, with just my instincts to guide me, I shopped around awhile—quite awhile—and finally found a two-family house I wanted.

And thus my career began.

How surprised I was when I discovered that I loved the process. I found it challenging and exciting. So I figured out how to use that first property to get my next property, and the next, and the next, and so on. After my first few properties, I elected to make real estate a full-time endeavor.

Within two years—though I had no experience, contacts, or training—I turned what was in effect a zero-dollar real estate investment into well over a million. That led me to found ORE International, a multinational real estate investment company. If all this sounds like a whirlwind of growth and activity—well, it was. These days, in addition to running my own business, I enjoy leading others to wealth as a private consultant to real estate investors at all levels and as a presenter to international corporations and high-net-worth individuals. I have also discovered different and imaginative ways to give back to my community. For example, some of my properties are used to provide homes for people living with HIV, and they are some of the tenants I am most proud to have.

Not bad for someone who was not exactly typical real estate investor material. But then, who is? Well, actually, *everyone*. In truth, there is no "typical" real estate investor. I see this just by looking at the people who attend my seminars all over the world. Everyone has the potential to make money from property investment.

## What's So Magical About Real Estate?

Real estate has never been hotter. And at no time in the history of real estate investment has the market been better positioned for the average Joe to take advantage of it. The facts are delicious . . . and staggering:

- More than 76 percent of American millionaires earned their wealth through real estate.
- Real estate has a 50-year history of appreciation. *Every 10.2 years, real estate values have doubled.*
- Real estate has been returning a profit of better than 10 percent. Combine this figure with the tax benefits of owning real estate and the return can jump to 35, 100, even 300 percent. (Just remember that—as the commercials say—past performance does not guarantee future returns.)
- You get more for your dollar: You can buy a million dollars' worth of real estate for $100,000. If your investment goes up by 10 percent, you haven't made 10 percent profit—you've made 100 percent profit. *Yes, 100 percent profit.*
- Real estate gives investors the power of leverage: You can use the equity of one property to buy another . . . and another, and another.

- The tax benefits are tremendous. One small example: An individual can sell his or her primary residence after having lived there for two years, profit up to $250,000, and pay no capital gains tax. For a married couple, that exemption jumps to $500,000. That's half a million dollars—tax-free—*every two years*.
- Mortgage rates are at an all-time low, and banks are competing fiercely for borrowers.

Real estate is open to anyone, no matter what your experience or how small your starting budget may be. And unlike stocks, the value of your property isn't affected by corporate or investment house corruption. Real estate gives you, the investor, greater control over your investment: A lick of paint, some flower boxes, or feng shui-ing the furniture could potentially increase the value of your property to a prospective buyer. That's the magic of real estate.

## But How Do You Do It?

I can't tell you how many times people have told me that some book they read on real estate investment left them inspired but confused about how to start investing. This is because most books on this subject—which are often written by people who studied real estate investment at school before becoming practitioners—are filled with amazing facts and theory, but very little practical guidance.

I did not learn about the real estate industry in the classroom, but rather hands-on: in the field, playing the game, talking to real estate industry professionals, and making lots of mistakes. This book is the condensed product of all my professional experience and success.

I travel extensively, leading seminars across the United States as well as in Europe and the Middle East. The response from people who attend my public seminars and follow my advice has been so positive that I know my program gets results. Because I started out in this industry with no insider info, I know what kind of inspiration and knowledge you've been searching for but have been unable to find. While reading The Real Estate Millionaire, you will come out in the field with me. You will join me as I scout potential properties to buy. You will see how I conduct negotiations. Through my example, you will gain the skill to work out your own unique approach to real estate investment. The lessons are written to help real estate investors of all levels: from the first-time home buyer to the professional eager to find ways to earn seven or eight figures.

*The Real Estate Millionaire* motivates you to take immediate action. We'll begin with a basic, ground-level explanation of the benefits of real estate investment, and then walk together through every aspect of the enterprise. At the end of each chapter, you'll find exercises that show you how to practically apply the principles introduced and further focus your goals. The last chapters of the book deal with how to maintain your success and expand your horizons beyond your wildest dreams.

Most importantly, through completing the activity sections at the end of every chapter, you will gain the confidence to put into practice what I have taught you. Even before you've finished the book, you'll be ready to take your first step.

## So Let's Get Started!

I recommend that you read *The Real Estate Millionaire* in its entirety first. You can then refer to the individual chapters and the chapter activities to help you identify solid investments as you go out in the field on your own.

Ultimately, don't hesitate to use this book at any point while investing in your properties—or to e-mail me at Boaz@OREinternational.com should you need more detailed advice on a specific property-investment-related issue. To find out more about ORE International's property ownership and management services, log on to www.OREinternational.com.

I wish you the best as you make your dreams come true. Please share them with me at www.realestatemillionaire.com.

Good luck!

—Boaz Gilad

# The Real Estate Millionaire

# 1

# The Power of Real Estate

## Passive Income, Passionate Life

We all love the idea of *having* money, but how many of us love the idea of *making* money? How many people actually wake up in the morning with the thought, *By the end of the day today, I'm going to have a thousand dollars cash in my hand?* If you're one of those rare people who is driven purely by the idea of making money, starting up in real estate investment may be easier for you than for others. But if you're not, let's look for the pathway that will connect your passions to real estate.

Perhaps it's difficult to believe that there could be a connection between making a lot of money and doing something you love. But know this: You aren't going to be successful at something if you're not passionate about it. Look at the people you admire—your favorite athletes, politicians, or artists. Inevitably these people are fixed on a goal, immerse themselves wholly in what they do, and pursue their passions with an amazing single-mindedness.

So what does that have to do with real estate? Ask yourself, *What am I passionate about?* You may not be a person who can get deeply excited about buildings—and that's fine. But what does turn you on? Perhaps it's your family, your pastimes or creative outlets, your house of worship, or your community—your friends or colleagues. When I started in real estate investment, acting was what turned me on. Like most of my peers, I was a *poor* actor—financially poor, that is. But my passion for the arts made me want to find a way to be able to pursue performing without having to constantly worry about how to make ends meet. That was what pushed me to take control of my financial destiny.

And I have. It's completely incidental that along the way I discovered an authentic passion for real estate. At first, I created that passion because I could see the long-term benefits. Namely, I could see the freedom that real estate ownership could supply by creating passive income.

What is **passive income**? It's money that you don't have to work for; rather, it works for you. A quick example: Say you have a real estate investment—a two-family house—whose expenses total $1,000 a month. From the rental income, you receive $3,000 a month. The difference is your passive income: $2,000 per month, or $24,000 a year. If you have five properties like this, the passive income is $120,000 a year. That's money that you *didn't have to spend time working for*. Imagine the hours you would have to put in working for someone else to earn that much—if you even had the opportunity to do so.

**passive income:** Money you don't have to work for.

This is where your life transforms. You're no longer working for money. It's working for you. Passive income is what will allow you to spend your time as you choose—pursuing whatever your passions dictate. And because the need for housing is a constant, having a sturdy property in place will ensure that you have a steady stream of **revenue** coming in. What will you do with the time and resources you've created for yourself?

**revenue:** Cash flowing in to you.

# The Magic Word That Turns
# One Property into Five

So how do you create passive income quickly? Welcome to the wonderful world of leverage. Leverage is the single most powerful concept in real estate investing. It will increase your potential and lead to your success faster than any other vehicle in the world.

> **leverage:** Increased power through the use of borrowed money.

It's as simple as this: You can buy $250,000 worth of real estate for $25,000. In other words, you can take advantage of a great deal of someone else's money using only a little bit of your own. And even more amazingly, you immediately get to benefit from a real estate investment's total cash value, even though you haven't invested anywhere near the full purchase price. (Even with that rare property where you make a zero down payment, you can still capitalize on the value as if you owned it outright.)

> **down payment:** The portion of the full purchase price that is not part of the mortgage.
>
> **equity:** The money value of a property.
>
> **refinance:** To reorganize the financing of a property by taking out a new loan.
>
> **home equity line of credit (HELOC):** A mortgage on your home that operates like revolving credit. You may borrow none, a portion, or all of the available credit based on your needs.
>
> **asset:** Something of value that is owned.
>
> **collateral:** Something of value given as security for a loan.
>
> **default:** Failing to fulfill a legal agreement.

Leverage is the magic word that turns that property into five. Because you can capitalize on the value of the entire investment, you can use the equity in your first property to purchase your next one. Banks are happy to give you money through refinancing or a home equity line of credit. (There's a lot more about this in Chapter 5, "Cold Hard Cash.") Banks know that real estate is one of the most stable and dependable assets that exists in the world. If they loan money to a homeowner, they have a great source of collateral in the event that the homeowner defaults on the loan. In contrast, try getting a loan against stocks or bonds.

You use the cash that the bank hands you from your first property to buy a second one. Then guess what? The banks will be thrilled to give you a loan on property number two. What do you do with that money? You buy another property. And so on, and so on, and so on. I like to imagine an ancient pharaoh building a pyramid. Your first property is your first stone. You dig it up and place it in the desert. Then you fit your next stone—or next property—right against the first. Each stone matches up exactly with the previous one. Pretty soon you step back and take a look at the big picture—and find you're halfway to building your own monument.

## Appreciating Appreciation

Now this is where investment gets really good. Unlike other investments whose value can fluctuate tremendously, real estate has a 50-year history of appreciation. Its pattern has been to go up in value for six to seven years, level off, dip a bit, and then start its trend of increasing again. History shows that every 10.2 years, real estate values have doubled.

This great track record makes the bank very comfortable and works to the real estate investor's advantage in several ways. Let's say you purchased a $250,000 property, using $225,000 of the bank's money. After a year, the property is worth $280,000—it has increased in value by $30,000. You originally put 10 percent down on the property, so does this mean your investment has increased over 10 percent? Nope. It means that your $25,000 investment has returned *better than 100 percent*—in one year!

> **appreciation:** An increase in value over time.
> **mortgage:** A written agreement that creates a **lien** against property as security for a debt.
> **lien:** A claim against a property. A lien gives a creditor the right to take a property if you don't pay a debt. Liens can

be consensual (including mortgages and home equity loans) and nonconsensual (including liens for unpaid taxes and contractors).

So now you go back to the bank, politely point out that the value of your property has increased by $30,000, and tell them you'd like to refinance the mortgage. The bank will hand over $27,000. (Why wouldn't the bank give you the full $30,000? Because it will always require that you leave at least 10 percent of the value in the property—in this case, $28,000, or your initial $25,000 plus $3,000 from the increase.) Still, you own a $280,000 property with essentially none of your own money left in it. In short, we appreciate appreciation!

# Did You Know about *All* These Tax Benefits?

Tax benefits. Sounds like an oxymoron, right? You may hate taxes now, but in Real Estate Land, they are beautiful and kind. Tax benefits are what can transform your 10 percent profit into 35, 100, even 300 percent.

Why would the government extend any tax benefits for homeownership? Simple. Uncle Sam *likes* it when the American people buy homes. Homeownership is good for the stability of the economy, so the fine folks in Congress and the IRS have created some beautiful perks—some real, some they dreamed up—to encourage home buying. And since the real estate lobby in Washington, D.C., is extremely powerful, chances are these tax benefits won't be going away anytime soon.

## The Half-Million-Dollar Handout

Here's a simple tax benefit available to every homeowner who pays taxes: In 1997, Congress passed the Exclusion Act, which applies to property sales after May 6, 1997. This law states that in the United States, you can live for a minimum of two years in a primary residence, sell the residence for a profit, and keep up to $250,000 of that profit *tax-free*. That amount jumps to $500,000 for a married couple. (Hey, if you're single and are looking at a $500,000 profit, you might want to find a spouse fast.) You can then go buy another home, live there for two years, and do the same thing. If you've lived in your home for less than two years but sell it due to unforeseen circumstances—say, a change in employment—you can even get a partial exclusion. Now say, *"Thank you, Uncle Sam, for saving me the 15 percent capital gains tax that I would pay if I made that money on any other kind of investment."*

**capital gain:** Profit on the sale of an asset.
**capital gains tax:** Tax paid on the profit.

### Capping the Cap

The maximum capital gains tax rate for long-term (one-year-plus) capital investments is 15 percent. However, there is a 25 percent rate that applies to the gain on the sale of real estate that you have depreciated in prior years, and to other real estate held and sold in business or trade. Check with your lawyer or accountant for the full scoop on how tax benefits apply to you and your properties!

### *Mortgage Interest*

Let's imagine it's January 1975, and you're buying your first home. Your banker is pleased as punch to be offering you a 30-year fixed mortgage. He'll give you a $50,000 mortgage on your $60,000 house, and you'll pay it off slowly. Each monthly payment will be a combination of mortgage **principal** and **interest**.

**principal:** The base amount of the loan owed.
**interest:** The fee paid for borrowing money.

In the first month, approximately 99 percent of your payment will be applied to the interest on the loan. Why? Because the bank doesn't want you to pay into the principal before it's made its profits. So the sliding scale over time gradually flips. Your final mortgage payment in January 2005 is 99 percent principal, 1 percent interest. (See Figure 1.1.)

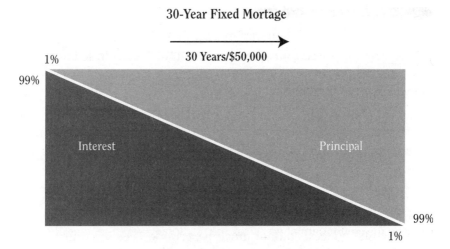

**Figure 1.1.** Mortgage graph for standard 30-year fixed mortgage.

---

### Quick Tip

I don't necessarily advocate a 30-year mortgage in today's market. By the time you've finished paying that $50,000 mortgage at a rate of 7 percent, you'll have handed the bank $380,612.75. When interest rates are extremely low, however, a 30-year fixed is not a bad idea for an investment property that you know you'll want to hold for a long time.

---

The 30-year mortgage here provides a simple example of some more good news for you: *Every penny of the mortgage interest you pay is tax-deductible.* Every penny of it. Thanks again, Uncle Sam.

---

### Insider's Tip!

Thirty-year mortgages were created at a time when people took "jobs for life" and retired with a gold watch and a party. I take three-year interest-only mortgages on many of my properties: My entire mortgage is tax-deductible, and I don't waste a dime on paying off the principal. (More on this in Chapter 5, "Cold Hard Cash.")

---

## Home Equity Happiness

The baby-boomer generation was brought up with the idea that paying off a 30-year mortgage was a great achievement. (And it was.) In addition, these days many boomers are apprehensive about their future because they have stopped working and their money isn't working for them. With both these thoughts coloring their sensibility, they're now sitting in houses, mortgage-free, worth hundreds of thousands of dollars, yet doing nothing with the equity. They are understandably hesitant to take out another mortgage. Enter the home equity line of credit.

A home equity line of credit is like a checkbook against the value of your primary residence. Many banks will be happy to open one for you with no closing costs, no fees, and not much paperwork. Let's say your home is worth $500,000, with a mortgage paid in full. The bank will give you an open credit line of $400,000. What does Uncle Sam take out of that $400,000 that just came into your world? You guessed it. *Nothing*.

You can do what you like with the money. You could buy a yacht or a fleet of luxury cars—but please don't! Of course, I advocate buying an investment property. Besides being a profit-making venture, you can use the money you gain from a good investment to make the payments on your home equity loan. But just the interest! *Why not pay the principal, too?* you ask. Because the money is cheap, and it's working for you. Don't ruin a good thing.

## Appreciating Depreciation

Depreciation is an idea completely invented by the government that extends to *all* ownership property—your primary home and any investment properties. Why would they just make something up? Simple. You already know why: The government *likes* it when the American people buy homes.

> **depreciation:** The reduction in the value of a property expressed as a deduction for income tax purposes.

Uncle Sam decided that everything inside your home needs to be replaced every 30 years or so. Everything. Big appliances, like refrigerators and stoves, are valued at a seven-year depreciation. Other items are deductible over longer periods of time; these include the windows and even the wiring that you've never seen inside the walls! So every year at tax time, homeowners are allowed to write off a portion of all the "replaceables" in their homes. That's a hefty tax deduction, invented by the government, just for your benefit.

### The 1031 Tax Exchange

Okay, let's jump ahead a bit. Imagine you're not just a homeowner; now you're a real estate investor. You have 2, or 3, or 10 properties. You want to sell one, but it isn't your primary residence, so you can't use the Exclusion Act. What does your favorite uncle do for you now?

The 1031 (ten-thirty-one) Tax Exchange is named after the tax code in which it's found—romantic, huh? This tax code allows you to get on the next rung of the property ladder. Here's how it works: After you sell a property, you purchase another property at equal or greater value. If a 1031 exchange is effected and used within five months, *no capital gains taxes are collected on any amount of the purchase price*. Read that sentence again. It can revolutionize your possibilities.

---

### Insider's Tip!

You can use the 1031 Tax Exchange when you sell your primary residence if your profits total more than $500,000. If you use this wisely—combined with the Exclusion Act or half-million-dollar handout—you should never have to pay a penny of capital gains tax on the sale of your primary residence.

---

Let's look at an example. Suppose you bought an investment property (*not* a primary residence) in 1998 for $100,000. The neighborhood improved, and property values increased. By 2005, the neighborhood is so thriving that someone offers you a ridiculously high price for the house— more money certainly than the bank **appraisal** of it. Let's say the buyer offers you $500,000. You have a capital gain of $400,000. If you simply sell the property, you'll owe the government a 15 percent capital gains tax, about $152,000. But good investors know better. Instead, you find another property that's for sale at $500,000 or more, and you pay for that property with the $500,000 you just received for your first property. Now you can keep that $152,000—you owe *no* capital gains taxes.

> **appraisal:** A professional opinion of a property's value.

For a brief moment, of course, that $152,000 is tied up in your new property; you can't spend it. *Yet.* Because here's what you do: You call the bank and let them know that you own a half-million-dollar property with no mortgage. See how quickly they jump to give you one. And refinancing a mortgage is . . . remember . . . *tax-free!*

## Leading a Rich Life: Important Things Not to Lose Sight Of

Real estate investment used to be accessible only to a privileged few—those who had wealth or relationships with powerful individuals or bankers. But the tide has turned and the secret is out. Enthusiasm over real estate is everywhere. There are real estate investment books, seminars, and brokers willing to work on every level with investors. Why? Because at no time in the history of real estate investment have all the factors been better aligned for the average individual to benefit.

In addition to being a great investment for your future, real estate (unlike, say, the stock market) can give you the chance to give back to people you care about. I constantly make sure that I am aware of the privileged life I have: I make a lot of money, do a job I'm proud of, and serve and help others through my business. It's important to ask yourself, *How can real estate help me?* and *How can I help others through real estate?*

*Come on,* you may think. *I'm not interested in helping others. I just want to make a buck.* But take a moment to consider whom that attitude serves. Has it served the big moneymakers? Certainly not the executives of Enron or WorldCom. Real estate is about service to people, bettering other people's lives *while* you are bettering your own. If you move beyond the "only-for-money" mindset, you will realize even greater financial windfalls for yourself.

I provide properties that people are proud to live in. I go the extra mile and never forget that these are people's homes: I put flower boxes in the windows as a housewarming. I bring in a professional cleaning service the day before move-in. At holiday time, I present each tenant with a card and a coupon good for a reduction in the January rent, thanking them for being tenants. For me, it's no more than a few hundred or thousand dollars (and it's a good end-of-the-year tax deduction), but some of the letters of thanks I receive from tenants are extraordinary. And my tenants keep their homes in better shape, they stay longer, and they recommend their friends to live in my vacant properties during soft rental markets.

> **soft market:** A market that features an oversupply of something and subsequent low demand for it.

There are also many programs already established that you can find and become a part of to better your community. My personal favorite not-for-profit organization helps me provide housing in my buildings for people who are HIV-positive. These tenants are among the best I've ever had. They respect the properties and take wonderful care of their homes. So I feel great about giving back to the community, and at the same time I'm making a living, a great living.

A rich life begins with relationships—with your tenants, with your investors, and with your entire team. Partnership is very important. So nurture your connections. The way for you to succeed is to keep creating bigger and bigger waves out there, so people *know what you're up to*. Make people *want* to know what you're up to. Don't create enemies. Don't be stingy.

Be responsible and generous to the people around you. It will strengthen your own commitment. If you raised $25,000 from your friends and family to begin investing, don't ever forget that. You've got to be responsible with their money because they trusted you at the start. You knew nothing about real estate, and they were willing to take a big risk and help you. It's better to lose your money first than their money. Your name is more important than your profit. (More on this in Chapter 9, "Maintain Your Success.")

It's all about being generous. You want to be someone who sleeps soundly at night, not feeling that you've made money to the detriment of others. It's my intent that you, as a real estate investor, be proud of what you do.

## So What's Stopping You?

I just handed you the keys to a brand-new life—and one that doesn't include the same old job day after day. It doesn't include buying lottery tickets and praying for your magic numbers to come up. It doesn't include betting your life's savings on a hot stock tip. And it doesn't break the law in any way.

What does it do? Here's some food for thought:

- Real estate gives you the opportunity to build your own business, without having to plunk down a fortune—sometimes without having to plunk down *anything*.
- It provides roofs over the heads of everyone who has ever needed one. (And that's just about everyone.)
- It sustains good communities and creates better ones.
- It allows you the possibility of walking away from your J-O-B—Just Over Broke—and frees you from ever again having to work for someone else.

You can concoct a million excuses for why you can't take the leap: fear of the unknown or risk, not having the money or time, or not understanding the numbers or laws. These are all understandable concerns, but as you work your way through each chapter in this book, I challenge you to confront these excuses. As you learn more and more about the realities and possibilities of real estate investment, I think you'll find these concerns slowly falling away. "Get-rich-quick" is a fantasy. But real estate has provided thousands of people with "get-rich" reality. Are you ready to join us? Then do what so many people are scared to do: Turn the page and get in action.

## Action Points: Stepping into Your New Identity

1. Many of us have ideas about what it means to make a lot of money or what it is to be a real estate investor. Some of those ideas may be neg-

ative. This activity helps you begin to reimagine what it means to be a person with wealth.

What associations do you have with the terms *real estate investor* or *real estate*? Complete these statements as quickly as possible.

Real estate investors are _____ .

Real estate investors are _____.

Real estate investors are_____.

Real estate investors are_____.

Now rewrite any negative associations you may have into positive ones. For example, if you wrote "real estate investors are crooks" change it to "real estate investors are honest."

Self-talk is a powerful thing. If you assume that real estate investors are crooks—if the word *crooked* comes up in your mind whenever you think about investing—this assumption will color your commitment to your new passion, and could color the kind of investor you turn out to be. Simply turning around your associations, however, can actually help create a new reality.

2. When we're feeling afraid about starting something new, often it's because we have fears and criticisms lurking in our past that disempower us. This activity helps you begin to set aside negative messages you may have received.

Think back over your life and list three people who have criticized or sabotaged your sense of potential or people you'd like to prove something to. What did they say that has affected you badly?

1. _____

2. _____

3. _____

Again, turn the messages around. For example if you wrote, "My parents told me that my family has bad luck with money," change it to "I am a person who is lucky with money."

Simply changing your beliefs about yourself can change your *self*. It works!

# 2

# Identify Your Niche

At this point you might be thinking, *Okay, I get the why of real estate; now I just need to understand the* how. But before you can delve into the details of making deals, you need to figure out *who you are* as a real estate investor. Where do you want to buy? For whom? What kind of buildings? What role do you want to play in your business? By the time you finish reading this chapter, you'll be able to identify your niche in the world of real estate investment.

Knowing your niche is critical to your success in this field. We'll spend a lot of time talking about this. So what *is* a niche, anyway?

Your niche encompasses two elements:

1. **What do I have to offer the business of real estate?** What passions, skills, and values do I bring to this field?

2. **What do I already know about real estate?** That is, what customers and what kinds of properties do I understand best—consciously or unconsciously?

Discovering your niche will begin to shape your business and ensure your success.

## You Already Know Your Market, Too

When it comes to real estate investment, is one of your first thoughts, *Who, me?* Well, me too. I lived in New York for six years before entertaining the possibility of being a property owner—six years of tiny apartments in less-than-desirable neighborhoods, six years of loaning my couch to new actors in town, six years of scrambling around when a lease was about to expire. I wasn't a businessman; I was an actor—and I didn't even like the business parts of my career.

But in a way, my skills were apparent all along. When the rent was due or the mice got too friendly, I was always the one elected to go chat with the landlord. My greatest strength has always been my ability to talk with people—all people, from any background, from any position along the economic scale. It took me a while to realize it, but verbal communication—and my genuine enjoyment of people—is my greatest real estate asset.

Real estate investment is a huge, sprawling field that encompasses (or perhaps I should say *requires*) countless specialized activities. The thing is, it's also a field where you get to choose which of those activities to focus on. It comes down to your inclinations. You find the parts that excite you and use your skills, then find a way to work around the ones that excite you less or don't come quite as naturally. You do this because *you* are the one in control.

How do you figure out which elements of real estate investing are going to get you energized? At the end of this chapter, you'll find an exercise that will enable you do exactly that.

## Investment and the Niche

You want to know the hottest real estate market right now? In most places, you can hardly say the word *investment* out loud without someone telling you where you should be looking. It's always the most amazing up-and-coming neighborhood. Or else it's the hidden enclave that no one knows about. How do all these would-be matchmakers know what works for you? While they're telling you to put up your money, all they're putting up is an opinion. This isn't so different from being set up on a blind date . . . it just has potentially more devastating consequences. Taking "hot market" advice from anyone else is a big risk. So stop looking around. *Because the hottest real estate market—right now—is the one you already know best.*

Real estate is not just about buildings or bricks, or what or where to buy. It's about meeting real human needs. And here's the point: You inherently understand your own needs, and the needs of your community. No doubt you've spent a good portion of your life seeking out places you fit in—places that you feel comfortable, where you intuitively know the rules, and where you belong. Places where you can use your skills, do what you do best, and be valued for it. Communities in which the people around you share your passions and center their lives on the same values you do. This is your niche (or niches—we all play many roles in life).

*You're already an expert.* You can compete in the real estate marketplace because when you start with what you know and love, you don't *have* to compete in the traditional sense. Instead, you tap into, or even create, a market that isn't even recognized.

> *Dan was considering buying a building, but there was a lot of competition—more experienced players were getting the sales. How could he compete?*
>
> *Dan looked at his skills, passions, and values. As the owner of a technology company, he realized quickly that high-tech is his niche—it's what he loves and what he's best at. So when he entered the real estate marketplace, he tapped into this by buying himself an old building very close to the campus of a technical college. He then rewired the phone and cable system to provide Internet connections; he also peppered wireless routers throughout the building, to let students work on their laptops from anywhere.*
>
> *When Dan put his apartments on the market, he was able to rent them at above market value. His tenants knew they could get their work done (and check out the online personals) anytime day or night. They appreciated the proximity to school, too.*

# The Real Estate Millionaire

*Dan used his knowledge and life experience as a leverage tool in real estate. And as you make your way in the world of real estate, you're going to find lots of ways to do the same.*

Countless aspects of your experience and lifestyle have given you substantial expertise in where and how the people you know want to live. Here's the fundamental question: Which group of people do you know best? What groups do you belong to, effortlessly? These are the people you will serve best.

---

### By the Way . . .

If you averaged out your five closest friends' annual salaries, you'd probably find your own to be in the same ballpark. Why? Because generally we spend our time with people who have the same status, values, and needs as we do.

---

In my case, I wanted my first properties to serve the community I knew: actors. What did I know about actors' lives? Well, actors' professional lives take place in Manhattan—auditions, Broadway and off-Broadway, late-night restaurant jobs, temp agencies, and day jobs. But Manhattan real estate is prohibitively expensive, so I knew that neither I nor my community could afford it. To find the right properties, then, I opened the New York Transit subway map. I drew a large circle on the map to encompass areas no more than 10 stops away from Manhattan in any direction. Next, I began to eliminate neighborhoods. First, any that were too expensive were crossed out. Then any properties more than a five- or six-block walk from the subway got the "X," too. (Actors' schedules too often call for late-night subway trips.) What I was left with might have been a bit gritty, but I also knew these actors wouldn't stay in any one apartment for long, and wouldn't be raising kids there, so I didn't disqualify any neighborhoods. All these factors led me easily to the areas that I knew would suit my customers.

After several more steps (coming up in later chapters), I acquired buildings in these neighborhoods. I simply placed an ad in the actors' newspaper, *Back Stage*: "Providing housing for actors by actors." I instantly had an exclusive pool of tenants to draw from. There was no competition because my ad was the only one of its kind in the entire paper.

*Gustavo's experience is another example of how your knowledge and values can help you create a niche. When Gustavo used this chapter's exercise to look at what's most important to him in life, he realized one of his top five values was environmental conservation.*

*Gustavo was in the fortunate position of having the means to build new buildings, but here's how recognizing his niche impacted him: Rather than building what he calls "McMansions"—large houses that eat up forestland and resources—he found an architect to design homes that harmonize with nature. They're sited in ways that preserve wildlife and trees, and their power and water systems are all environmentally friendly. That's his thing.*

*Moreover, Gustavo was already a part of a community of folks committed to the environment. They were fellow members of the organizations he belonged to, they read the magazines he subscribed to, and they frequented the stores where he did his shopping. Gustavo instinctively knew what features these people wanted in their homes; he knew how to find these people, and how to market to them, too. Now they're his customers.*

Here's an analogy that might help you grasp the "niche" concept: Think about a lighthouse that stands motionless and emits its light. Those boats that need the light are attracted to it; those that don't simply sail on by.

When it comes to real estate, many of us act like we're stranded on an island, running up and down the beach trying to attract the boats to us. We've all seen enough movies to know that this just doesn't work. Find your niche and business will come to you. A "jack-of-all-trades, master of none" mentality will wear you out when you've barely begun—just as it wears out so many would-be real estate investors. Instead, let people be attracted to the confidence and natural expertise that your niche provides.

Identifying your niche based on what you already know will separate you from the crowd and give you an instant advantage as well as a much higher level of success. And remember, you don't need to spend the rest of your life investing only in those properties. Start there. After you make your first million dollars, you can always explore other markets.

## What Happens If You Don't Know Your Niche?

The Sun Belt of the United States has become the newest frontier in real estate investing, and I've been out there on several occasions to investigate the market. Offers of "no money down" and "100 percent return" abound in the Southwest. So I took one company up on their offer to show me the town and its best investments.

"Roy," the real estate broker, picked me up in his air-conditioned SUV and drove me to a brand-new development to show me the model homes. He led me up outdoor steps to a sweeping entranceway. An ornate chandelier hung from a high, vaulted ceiling. "Feast your eyes on the marble floors and fireplace," he announced proudly.

Roy led me up the curved stairway to a stunning master bedroom suite. As we admired the upscale amenities, he told me that Vegas is the fastest-growing retirement community for baby boomers. They wanted to sell this home to me as an investment, and in many ways it *was* very attractive. I began to fantasize about moving my parents, recent retirees, to this luxurious residence. Roy invited me to buy in at **phase one**, based solely on the plans before construction began. By the end of construction I would "make a fortune," he insisted, on the increase in value and price. "Let's head over to the office and sign the contract before all the units are gone," Roy proposed. I pictured myself, bursting with pride, showing Dad my incredible investment and gift for him . . .

> **phase one:** The first phase of a project. For a new development, this phase occurs before building begins.

Now let's rewind this movie. At the entrance to the house, there were *three steps* up to the front door. The beautiful marble stairs led to a *second floor*. At the same time, my new friend Roy kept referring to "baby boomers" flooding Vegas as a retirement community—selling their homes on the East Coast and using the proceeds to buy into these luxury new homes.

I'll admit that I know very little about the needs of aging baby boomers. Still, if I think for even a moment about this niche, it strikes me that one of their prime concerns must be accessibility. Over the next 10 or 20 years, boomers are likely to need physical assistance. Some will depend on walkers, wheelchairs, or assistants; others will simply find their movements circumscribed by pain and infirmity. So what in the world were those first three entranceway steps doing in a potential retiree home? At best, they'd be an inconvenience; at worst, they could be insurmountable. And could a wheelchair fit into the narrow doorways of the bathrooms? How would that wheelchair ascend the (admittedly stunning) grand staircase? Marble flooring, moreover, is bad news indeed in case of a fall.

If I hadn't known real estate, I could have easily been duped by Roy and his polished presentation. The bottom line is, if you don't know the needs of a given niche, you will not be successful at serving those people—or yourself.

My experience in the Vegas desert is actually pretty common; I've talked to a lot of would-be real estate investors who've been offered the same slick air-conditioned tours of the booming market in Tampa or Phoenix. Yes, those markets have been booming, but everything is booming now. The question you should ask yourself is, *Why are these hot areas?* In my experience, many of them only got that way because some big new developers turned their attention to making them hot.

Don't forget, every party will come to an end. Do you want to be the one to wake up with the hangover? You'll hear about awesome new investment areas wherever you go these days—over drinks at a wedding, in the pages of women's fitness magazines, from friends, acquaintances, and total strangers.

Here's something to think about: We are currently riding a real estate wave, very similar to the technology stock wave in the late 1990s. And the thing about waves is this: They break. If you've invested in a niche you know nothing about, however, you'll likely never recognize the danger signals. When the wave does break, you could well be the last one to jump ship.

---

## The Real Estate Cycle

As you ponder the balancing act between risk and responsibility in your investment career, here's a little something to think about:

In the United States, real estate values have historically been highly cyclical, and the average market cycle lasts seven years. Right now, as I write these words, real estate has been hot for *twelve years*.

Now, *how* much debt did you want to take on again?

---

Even more important: Unlike the stock market, you can't just log on to the Internet and dump the property you own. You must find a buyer; and that can take months or even years. When those hot markets start heading downhill—and they will—the only people who will benefit from the inevitable foreclosures are (surprise!) those same companies that sold you "the next hot area."

All of that said . . . keep an open mind. You may find your niche in an unexpected area.

*Duncan worked in a beleaguered San Francisco dot-com. As his company was going down, he watched the owners struggle to pay rent on their huge loft-style space. It was a great, trendy location, but a crippling financial burden.*

*When the firm finally went belly-up, Duncan found himself in the ranks of the newly unemployed. And as you can imagine, he wasn't alone: Joining him there were a lot of people who still had great ideas in the field of technology but couldn't afford offices for the companies they wanted to form.*

*When he looked around, it quickly dawned on Duncan that there was a real need out there. So he figured out how to meet it: He took a very large office space, split it into small offices that fit one or two people each, and hired a single receptionist out front to assist all 22 units. He used movable walls in case particular tenants wanted a larger or smaller space. He provided furniture, as well as phone and Internet connections. All that potential entrepreneurs had to do was show up with a laptop.*

*The offices were a huge success—even considering the fact that Duncan charged more than the standard (per-square-foot) rental fees, given each facility's flexibility and infrastructure.*

*How did Duncan know that he was offering something desirable—a hot property? Because he himself came from the high-tech industry. He found a way to serve the people he knew best.*

## The Greatest Niche: Community

I recently read, "You are truly rich when you serve as many people as possible." Ask yourself: *How can I serve my community? What can I provide for people that they really need?* If you find your niche while you're also making a contribution to your community or doing something you love, it will be that much easier for you to succeed, and that much more satisfying when you do.

In my case, I was looking to serve a community of folks in the same boat I'd occupied for so long: actors who often need to work out of town for weeks or months at a time. As I knew from personal experience, many end up paying the rent on their empty apartments while they're away, or risk violating their lease by subletting.

So I went to my attorney, and together we modified standard rental contracts in ways that allowed for flexible sublets. This freed my tenants from the burden of rent during their stints away. It was a way to meet a critical need of my tenants and, at the same time, make my property that much more attractive to potential new renters.

*Jenny was looking for a new investment in Arizona. She happened to be walking in Phoenix when she saw a disheveled boy step outside and stake a* FOR SALE *sign in his yard. Jenny immediately approached, hoping a parent was nearby so she could find out more about this property. She introduced herself to young John, who explained that his mother was a victim of domestic violence; John's dad was beginning a long prison sentence.*

*As a government employee, Jenny was already familiar with social programs that provided funding for domestic violence shelters. Inspired by John's fortitude, Jenny bought the place with the promise of turning it into a women's shelter. Phoenix House became the first of several women's shelters she created. She had found not just an investment but also a purpose, and she went on to make a tremendous difference in the lives of many.*

*Jenny's work experience—her niche—gave her the tools and the confidence she needed to make her investment dreams a reality.*

## To the Bricks and Mortar

So now that you have a new view of what real estate is *really* all about, let's turn for a moment to the actual buildings. And the good news here is, you already know something about the bricks and mortar of real estate, just as you're already an expert in your marketplace niche.

### Property Types

Consider all the places you've lived in your life, as well as places you've worked. Which of the following types of properties are you already familiar with?

- **Residential properties:**
  - Single-family homes
  - Apartments
  - Small multifamily buildings
  - Large (four or more units) multifamily buildings
  - Mobile homes
- **Retail properties:** Malls, strip malls, storefronts
- **Office properties:** Small, medium, vast, mixed
- **Industrial and manufacturing properties:** Auto repair shops, factories, warehouse centers
- **Mixed-use properties:** Retail, residential, industrial, and/or office spaces together

### Property Features

Now go back to thinking about the kinds of people you know best—your niche community, your customers, the folks you'll be serving. Any number of factors will be important to your tenants, of course, and it's impossible to predict all of them. Still, looking at your niche, and at the type of property you'd like to invest in, here are some things that your tenants may care deeply about. Take a look at these lists, and really consider which of these factors will be most crucial to your community. (These ideas are just a starting point. Hopefully they will spur other thoughts as you read through them.)

## For Residential Properties

### Community features:

- Multicultural/multigenerational or homogeneous—Are the neighbors of similar or different age or lifestyle? Are they singles; artists; couples with kids; empty nesters?
- Local politics—Is the area generally more liberal or conservative?
- Status or socioeconomic class—Is the area generally working class; professional; old money; mixed?

### Neighborhood features:

- Locale: urban/suburban/small town/rural

---

### Insider's Tip!

In rural and small-town areas, you'll get greater real estate results by taking an interest in the community. Never underestimate the power of small-town chatting!

---

- Crime rate
- Noise level
- Amount of street traffic
- Accessibility to public transportation
- Quality of school systems
- Availability of community services—police, fire, and ambulance services; hospitals; Neighborhood Watch or similar programs
- Garbage and recycling arrangements
- Availability of local services—supermarkets, pharmacies, banks, dry cleaners, post offices, libraries

- Types of shops and stores—discount stores, malls, funky shops; restaurants and coffeehouses
- Access to nature—parks, walkways, playgrounds, swimming and exercise areas
- Access to culture and entertainment—museums, theaters and other performance venues; nightspots and entertainment venues
- Access to health care
- Access to places of worship

## Home features:

- Desirable entrance arrangements—elevators/stairways (number and condition); lobby, doorman; private entrance; type and length of driveway
- Desirable layout—single- or multistoried; number of rooms; number of bathrooms; size of kitchen; attic/basement space; number of closets
- Infrastructure—age and condition of property; central heat and air; type and condition of plumbing, including water pressure; type and condition of wiring
- Outdoor access—yard, deck, balcony, rooftop

---

### Insider's Tip!

*Very new* and *very old* properties can be particularly appealing—depending, of course, on what shape they're in.

---

- Special features—you name it: garbage disposal; washer-dryer; dishwasher; garage or other parking arrangement; Internet access; cable or satellite TV; fireplace or woodstove; dog runs or doggy doors; bay windows or floor-to-ceiling windows; views

---

### Insider's Tip!

Animal-friendly rental homes and apartments are tougher to come by in many areas. You may be able to expand your niche if you are willing to accept pets.

---

# Identify Your Niche

## For Retail Properties:
- Square footage
- Number of entrances; separate delivery entrances
- Safety features—alarms, safety windows, grilles, sprinkler systems
- Bathrooms—for the public; for employees
- Garbage-collection arrangements
- Presence of competing stores
- Amount of traffic—foot traffic and/or vehicle
- Parking arrangements for customers; for staff
- Income level of surrounding neighborhood and its customer base
- Arrangements for (and restrictions on) signage or other advertising

## For Office Properties:
- Square footage
- Single- or multifloored
- Layout—Are there areas for conference rooms, break rooms, storage?
- Flexibility of workspace—can interior walls be added or removed?
- Does the space meet OSHA and ADA requirements?

**OSHA (Occupational Health and Safety Administration):** A federal agency that creates and enforces business health and safety regulations.

**ADA (Americans with Disabilities Act):** A federal civil rights law requiring that (among other things) landlords and employers must make reasonable accommodations to allow the disabled access to facilities.

- Entrance setup—private entry, stairs, or elevators; size and condition of lobby; entrance staff, including doormen, guards, receptionists, vendors
- Bathrooms
- Kitchen or kitchenette facilities
- Client/visitor facilities: bathrooms, parking, waiting rooms
- Electrical infrastructure—capacity of wiring, number and arrangement of outlets

- Internet infrastructure
- Telephone infrastructure
- Delivery and garbage arrangements
- Parking arrangements for staff; for clients
- Outdoor spaces for staff or visitors
- Potential for expansion
- Arrangements for (and restrictions on) signage or other advertising

## Commercial Real Estate

This book focuses largely on residential real estate—properties where tenants make their homes, including high-rises, condos, duplexes, individual homes, and so on. So what about commercial investment? What if your heart's desire is to open a retail mall, or an office building?

Commercial real estate can make for fabulous opportunities—but I advise against investing in the commercial arena when you're just starting out. That's why I haven't devoted much attention to it here.

If you're curious, however, here's the *good* news about commercial investment:

Commercial tenants sign generally long, *long*-term leases (several years or even longer), and they invest a lot of money in the property. A restaurant may need to install refrigeration, special venting, specialized ovens, and more. A white-collar firm might demand extra electrical wiring, high-speed cables, sophisticated lighting, and so on. When these tenants leave a property—when their long, long leases are up—they simply can't take all this stuff with them. So they leave it for you.

Sounds great, right? Well, here's the *bad* news:

After commercial tenants leave—and they will—you may go an equally long time before signing a new one. Signing your lease is a huge commitment for a company, and because of this you could find your property sitting empty for months while you find the right tenant and negotiate the right terms. Meanwhile, you'll be paying the mortgage and other expenses.

Even worse, if a commercial tenant chooses to move out at a moment when the economy is in a downturn, you could find your building empty for years. Commercial investors are deeply affected by economic conditions—far more so than residential investors. People always need a home; they don't always need a business space.

## For Industrial Properties:
- Square footage
- Single- or multifloored
- Layout—are there areas for offices, conference rooms, break rooms, storage?
- Flexibility of workspace—can interior walls be added or removed?
- Bathrooms
- Kitchen or kitchenette facilities
- Electrical infrastructure—capacity of wiring, number and arrangement of outlets
- Internet infrastructure
- Telephone infrastructure
- Does the space meet OSHA and ADA requirements?
- Delivery and garbage arrangements
- Parking arrangements
- Outdoor spaces
- Potential for expansion
- Arrangements for (and restrictions on) signage or other advertising
- Neighborhood—Is it appropriate for the industry?
- Zoning restrictions

## More Questions to Ask about Any Property
- Is the property prone to flooding? How sound is the basement?
- Is the property or area prone to any other natural disasters—hurricanes, erosion, mudslides, wildfires, tornadoes? How might this affect me, the investor, or my tenants?

- Are there any pending or recently approved plans in the works—for a new highway next door, underground fiber-optic installation along the avenue, zoning changes, building a nearby school, or the like?
- What is the area's potential for growth or deterioration over the next five years? Ten? Twenty?
- How is the property's structural integrity?
- What's the condition of the roadways surrounding the property?
- Is there any current (or potential) insect or rodent infestation? What pest-management practices have been followed in the past?
- How friendly are local officials to investors? How friendly are they to the particular industry I'm dealing with?

## Action Points: Finding Your Niche

The following exercise is critical to everything that follows in this book, and I urge you to read it through, think about it, and do the written work in a careful, unhurried way. Finding your niche is how you set yourself apart in the vast field of real estate investment, and how you avoid costly mistakes. Indeed, finding your niche is how you make sound and profitable judgments.

### Part 1: Your Passions

What are your passions in life? Here are some questions that will help you think about the things you love the most. As you read through them and write down your answers, think as broadly and creatively as you can. Let your mind range over every element of your life.

1. Think back on the last three jobs you've had—and think particularly about the actual tasks you performed. (You're looking here more at how you felt about the *work* you did than your feelings about your colleagues or workplace.) What experiences were most satisfying for you? Make a list of your three favorite moments in your working life.

   It's possible that a job or two provided you with no favorite moments. As I said, you'll want to think creatively here. If you strongly disliked a job, you probably had an idea of what should have made the tasks rewarding. Take a moment to fantasize, and write down those moments.

2. Think about how you've spent your free time recently—over, say, the last three years. Reflect on your activities and hobbies—the things you've done during evenings, weekends, or vacations. Write down your three favorite leisure-time memories.

3. Reflect on the conversations you've had recently. Are some more memorable than others? What are your top three subjects you enjoy talking about?

4. Think back on experiences that you remember as thrilling . . . exhilarating . . . mind-boggling. What are your three most exciting moments?

5. Finally, look at your relationships with the people you love: your spouse, children, family, and friends. What experiences left you feeling most connected with them—most loving and loved? List your three favorite people memories.

6. Now it's time to get even more creative. You should have 15 or so of your happiest, most treasured experiences listed. (It's fine if you have a few more or less. The point is to have a bunch.) Take a long, thoughtful look at these answers. What are the *patterns* or *common bonds* among them?

Here are some of the kinds of questions you might ask as you look through your responses. Did a lot of your favorite moments take place while you were alone—or while you were part of a team? Did they occur in the outdoors? Did they involve your imagination? Or maybe they involved your building skills . . . working under pressure . . . children, or animals . . . being the one in authority . . . words, or numbers, or images. Have you been happiest when moving around, or when sitting still? Are you more at home doing things, or talking about things?

As you work on this exercise, you might find that your common bonds are simple and obvious: *I love pounding nails* or *Music makes me happy*. But you might have to do some detective work and imaginative thinking, too. In the end, you'll have a list (maybe extensive, maybe very brief) of your passions. Call it *Stuff that Always Seems to Be around When I'm Happy*.

## Part 2: Your Skills

The next subject to consider is your talents. Where do your skills lie? What are you really good at? Ask yourself: *What do people come to me for advice about? What do I consider myself an expert in?* (I define *expert* as someone able to lead a 29 conversation on the topic.)

Discover your inner expert by thinking about the skill areas that follow. All of them are useful to real estate investment, by the way, and many of them are crucial. Which areas do you feel most at home in? Put a checkmark next to each area that you consider a strength:

- ❏ Administrative work
- ❏ Athletics
- ❏ Computers and technology
- ❏ Construction
- ❏ Conversation—the "gift of gab"
- ❏ Machinery
- ❏ Mathematics
- ❏ Nurturing (of children, animals, the disabled, what have you)
- ❏ Outdoor living
- ❏ Politics
- ❏ The law
- ❏ The performing arts: music, dance, theater
- ❏ The visual arts: sculpture, painting
- ❏ Sales
- ❏ Writing
- ❏ Other: _____
- ❏ Other: _____
- ❏ Other: _____

By the same token, you'll want to consider what you're *not* gifted at. I know that I could never be a building superintendent, for example, because I can't do handyman work. I simply never got the Mr.-Fix-It gene. Instead, I used my people skills to enlist, early on, a friend who's got a knack for repair and renovation.

As you move into the world of real estate, you are going to find ways to compensate for the talents you don't have. You'll find that one important way to offset those areas in which you are not an expert is by team building: establishing strong working relationships with people whose skill sets complement yours. We'll explore this subject in detail in Chapter 8, "Your Team."

## *Part 3: Your Values*

Finally, we're going to dig even deeper. Make a list of the five things in your life that are *most important* to you. This may take some time, and it's worth taking. Consider family, your kids' education, nightlife, being socially involved, the clubs or organizations you belong to, shopping, solitude, hobbies, and so forth.

It's important to be honest here. This isn't a list of things you *oughta* value (Being Kind to Baby Ducks, Giving the World a Hug); it's a list of things you *do* value—commitments you live out every day. If Having a Great Wardrobe or Buying That Great Truck is high on your value list, say so. Building a career around everything you *oughta* be will get you nothing but miserable.

As you consider your core values, try asking yourself questions like these:

- What do I love to do? (Here are your *passions* again.)
- What do I have that no one else has? What comes easily to me that others struggle with? (These are the *skills* you identified earlier.)
- Who are my friends? What do they have in common—in their lifestyles, their personalities, their ethics and values?
- Where am I in my life: Single with a busy social life? Half a young couple with a kid? Thinking about slowing down or retiring in the near future? What's most important to me in my living situation?
- What role does spirituality play in my life?
- What's my financial status? How badly do I want to improve it?
- If I won the lottery tomorrow, what's the first thing I'd do?
- What do I want my life to look like in ten years? Twenty?
- What do I want my children's lives to look like in ten years? Twenty?
- What do I most want to accomplish before I die?

These questions have nothing to do with real estate, but they have everything to do with real estate, because real estate is about people.

◆  ◆  ◆

You should now have three lists: your passions, your skills, and your values.

### Part 4: Putting It All Together:
### Where's the Real Estate in That?

So what do these lists have to do with your real estate investing career? This is a connection you'll start making now and continue making as you read this entire book. Here's how you to begin:

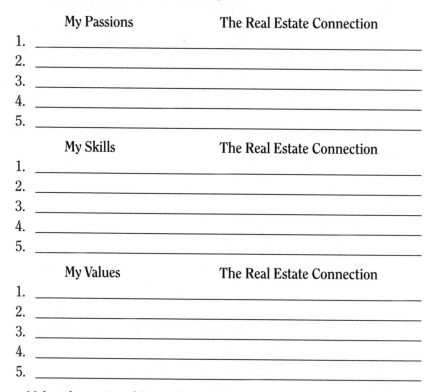

| My Passions | The Real Estate Connection |
|---|---|
| 1. | |
| 2. | |
| 3. | |
| 4. | |
| 5. | |

| My Skills | The Real Estate Connection |
|---|---|
| 1. | |
| 2. | |
| 3. | |
| 4. | |
| 5. | |

| My Values | The Real Estate Connection |
|---|---|
| 1. | |
| 2. | |
| 3. | |
| 4. | |
| 5. | |

Make a few copies of this exercise. Fill one out right now, as best you can. You may have to make some thoughtful, educated guesses as to all the activities that will be involved in a real estate career. Keep another copy of it with you as you continue reading, and fill it out whenever ideas strike you. Since this book will be taking you on a tour of the nuts and bolts of your new career, you'll want to do your exploring with all of your passions, skills, and values in mind.

# Identify Your Niche

To help spark your imagination and get you thinking, here are a few examples of how my students have completed this exercise.

| Passion | The Real Estate Connection |
|---|---|
| My golden retriever Joe | Offer pets-allowed apartments . . . add pet-friendly features (dog doors? dog runs? Lots of tile and washable surfaces?) |
| Numbers, math | Finding the best financial options |
| Civil War reenactment | Historic properties, authentically restored/furnished/maintained |

| Skill | The Real Estate Connection |
|---|---|
| I'm a great salesperson | Finding investors . . . finding tenants (maybe offer informational meetings?) . . . working with lenders |
| Woodworking | Offer customized cabinetry and built-ins to tenants . . . oversee contractors/interior designers |
| Details! | Guide loans and grants through to completion |

| Value | The Real Estate Connection |
|---|---|
| Getting my kids through college | Student housing |
| Shop till I drop! | Retail properties—malls |
| Support our troops | *Affordable* housing near military bases |
| Financial security | Be the deal maker, put investors together, put deals together, close the deal, get it done |

◆　◆　◆

Congratulations—you've just started thinking like an investor.

# 3

# Real Estate Begins at Home

Now it's time to put into practical application all the niche information you've just identified. And you're going to start by investigating specific *neighborhoods* and *areas*—not properties—that fall in line with the elements you've begun to identify as important to your niche, much as I did when I began exploring neighborhoods that would be appropriate for my actor community. As you're doing this detective work, you'll discover specific properties almost spontaneously.

In this chapter, you'll be guided to create a system of note keeping. By the end of the chapter, you will have created a viable list of potential investment neighborhoods and a way of tracking information about those areas.

## Targeting the Right Neighborhoods

*Church Avenue in Brooklyn, New York, is a very long street that arrows through the heart of the borough. It's a very bustling, hap-*

*pening place, with a lot of stores. For commercial space, it's very expensive. There's a Caribbean–West Indian community there. If you're from the West Indies, this is where you want to open a shop. It's hot.*

*One particular building along Church Avenue, however, was up for sale for a very long time. Every time I drove past, the FOR SALE sign was still in place. I was mystified. I thought,* It's a beautiful building. It's in a prime commercial location. There are three express trains close by. It's perfect. Why is this building not sold?

*So I went to one of the people I work with, a builder from Trinidad, and asked him about the property. He told me, "Oh, you can't touch this building."*

*I said, "Why?"*

*"This used to be a funeral home."*

*"Okay," I said. "And—?"*

*"No one from the West Indies or the Caribbean will walk in and buy something in a place that used to be a funeral home," he replied. "The spirits are still there."*

*Now, if I hadn't asked the right questions to someone who understood the neighborhood's culture, I might have bought this building. I would've put stores inside, and made it a great place to invest in. And absolutely no one in the neighborhood would have set foot inside.*

Real estate is about people. You need to know your niche and understand the needs of its people. When you start investing in real estate, you should begin with your niche and the people whose needs you already know how to serve. If I had been West Indian, I would have known that nobody on Church Street is going patronize a former funeral home. I would have just *known* to stay far away from that property. I was lucky to have found out. I saved myself a huge amount of money and heartache in the process. The lesson is to home in on the neighborhoods that fit the niche you're already an expert in.

And if you've read this far, you won't be surprised by what I have to say next: The key to finding the right neighborhoods is to connect with *information about people*, not information about real estate.

# Real Estate Begins at Home

So where do you start? There are a number of indispensable traditional and nontraditional sources for unearthing the right neighborhoods, but the key is to think like an investor. Once you have your real estate thinking cap on, there are infinite ways to sense the next hot neighborhood. Or even the next good, solid investment of a neighborhood.

## How to Read the Newspaper

You probably think you know how to use the newspapers for your investment research: You just flip to the for rent ads, or glance through the real estate stories for the next up-and-coming neighborhood. You should know, however, that if it's hot in the real estate section of the newspaper, it was probably "hot" five years ago. So while it's true that *eventually* you can glean some interesting information from the real estate section—namely, the availability and going rate for rentals in specific neighborhoods—you're not at that point yet. Still, a newspaper has a lot of even better stuff to offer you on your real estate journey.

Newspapers can give you a great sense of communities and neighborhoods. The City section of *The New York Times*, for instance, may never once mention real estate directly. But what it does have is feature stories about what's happening—and what's up and coming in specific areas across the city.

So let's say you sit down with the Sunday edition of your favorite paper. First, you read that someone has just opened a boys' and girls' club in Neighborhood X. Thinking like an investor, you say to yourself, *Wow. There must be a really strong sense of community in Neighborhood X. If this neighborhood fits into my niche, maybe I should check it out.*

Continuing through the City section, you learn that the mayor has just accepted a proposal for a large development in Neighborhood Y. Great! The development may not happen for years, of course, but real estate is a long-term investment. So you put Neighborhood Y on your list of locations to explore. Even if you know that the spot looks terrible right now—all factories and potholes—maybe it's got potential for change. Given the particulars of new development and a few years' time, will Neighborhood Y become a good match for your niche?

# The Real Estate Millionaire

Here's a real-life example of a great lead found by perusing the paper with purpose: One of my students, Mark, is 10 years my senior. After several consulting sessions, I determined that Mark's niche was young families with one or two kids. Next time we got together, over lunch, Mark produced an article from the local paper—a human interest story touting an energetic new principal in a middle-class district in Queens. This woman was so effective at her job that her students' standardized test scores had jumped nearly 10 percent. Mark's wife, Leanne, had circled the article with a big red marker and added, READ THIS, MARK!

"You want to move to Queens?" I asked him.

"Nope," he replied. "But I'll be out there scouting some property today."

He was right. Parents of young children are soon going to be flocking to that school district to provide their kids with a better education. Did Leanne read about this promising neighborhood in the real estate section? Not at all—this article was tucked inside the paper's B section. Anyone researching properties in all the usual ways would've missed it.

Thinking like investors, however, Mark and Leanne recognized the article for what it really was: a big green flag that spelled out GOOD INVESTMENT! GOOD INVESTMENT! Eventually the real estate section may "discover" this neighborhood, but by then, of course, it will be far too late—at least for the savvy investor.

## *Riding the Information Superhighway*

The Internet provides the same investigative value as local newspapers—except it's supersized. Plus, you don't even have to wait for a paper to arrive on your doorstep. You can also go online to search through older editions of newspapers, magazines, or what have you for insights into changes in a community—even one across the country.

You can start by visiting www.newspapers.com to find most any regional news site—or you can just type "news" and the city name into any search engine. Once you've found some good sites, try searching keywords like "human interest" or "community improvements"—anything related to people in the neighborhood. (*Not* "real estate"—not yet. Those searches will come later on, after you've focused on a specific location.)

You can also track neighborhood movement—how many people are moving in and out of a specific area—at all kinds of Web sites. Here are a few of them:

- www.realtor.com
- www.realestate.com
- www.homelistings-usa.com
- www.mls.com

---

### Insider's Tip!

Another useful Web site—both now and (especially) later on in your real estate search—is Realtrac.com. This site provides information on upcoming foreclosures, estate sales, and auctions. A 15-day free trial membership is available.

---

## *Word of Mouth*

Speaking of the Web, it certainly can be informative to peruse specific real estate agents' sites—as long as you recognize that by the time a property has arrived on a glossy Web site, *it has already been rejected by word of mouth* ("My cousin has a friend who's selling a house . . ."). Word of mouth will be your greatest ally when looking for your first investments. It's the first best thing to help you secure properties long before anyone else knows about them. And how do you encourage word of mouth? You talk. You tell everyone you know that you are a real estate investor and that you are seeking out investor properties. You'll be shocked how much information comes back at you. Like talking about the weather—everyone has something to say about property.

You're no doubt already starting to hear plenty of *have-I-got-a-tip-for-you!* suggestions if you're chatting people up. The trick is to distinguish the genuinely hot insiders' scoop from the unending stream of well-meaning but totally wrongheaded pointers. Take a look at the source and ask yourself: *Does this person live inside the community she's gushing over?* Also: *Does he have something to gain in this situation?* If you're talking to a real insider, you might want to pause and take note. If you're not—or if your adviser has a hidden agenda—nod, smile, and listen, cautiously. *But don't ignore.* You never know.

## Scouting the Right Neighborhoods

When I started out, my niche was housing for actors and artists. I already knew a lot about this market, but I needed to settle on a few specific neighborhoods to target. So I did my research—talking, listening, reading, scanning. I quickly realized that a lot of young people and artists seemed to be moving to Clinton Hill, a neighborhood in Brooklyn. So right away, I put Clinton Hill on my list of neighborhoods that bore further investigation.

Then I visited. I went to Clinton Hill and spent some time hanging out in the popular local coffee shops, meandering the streets and avenues, studying the signs posted on walls, lampposts, and bulletin boards, and striking up conversations wherever I could.

Once you have targeted a specific neighborhood that interests you, the next step is to check it out live and in person. There are two crucial pieces of information you're looking for in particular:

1. Does this neighborhood fit my niche?
2. What does this neighborhood's rental or sales market look like? Are there a lot of properties available, or very few? What are the price ranges of rentals and sales?

## The Five Senses

First things first: Is this neighborhood a good fit for you and your market? All the financial nuts and bolts can wait until you've answered this question. Your process of discovering the answers to this question should encompass all your senses: You need to see, hear, taste, smell, and feel what the neighborhood has to offer.

### See

So, you read an article about a particular area, or you heard about it from someone. You thought, *That seems like my niche. It could be a place I want to invest in*. Well, now it's time to put on the observation goggles. Get to know what's happening there. Sit in the coffee shops, stroll the sidewalks, visit the stores in the neighborhood. Look around and pay attention to everything you see.

## Real Estate Begins at Home

As I continued my research into Clinton Hill in Brooklyn, I biked the neighborhood at all different hours of the day—morning, midday, rush hour, whatever. Even at midnight, I'd get out the bike and go for a ride. (I didn't drive around at first, because I wanted to really be exposed to the area.) I wanted to see how people lived in Clinton Hill—what their lives were like. Were there folks hanging out on the corner selling drugs? Or selling lemonade? What kind of people got out of the subway at 9 or 11 P.M.? What I saw was a lot of people coming home from Manhattan late at night. *Perfect for my market*, I thought. *So what's it like at 8 A.M.?*

There I was, back on my bike in the early morning. This time I saw that hardly anyone was around. Quite a change from other New York neighborhoods—even those very close by—which are filled with a variety of blue- and white-collar professionals heading to work in the morning. In Clinton Hill, by contrast, I saw that it was generally 10 or 11 A.M. before residents started heading for the subway. *Okay*, I thought. *These have got to be younger people who wake up late and start their jobs late. It's that type of market.*

My careful look at Clinton Hill told me that my initial instinct was right: This could be a great spot for actors' housing. While it's slightly rough, actors won't be raising families there; they won't spend more than three or four years there. And as a group, actors tend to thrive in multicultural, multiethnic communities. This is what I mean when I advise you to see a neighborhood. See how the residents live, work, travel, relax. Be realistic about what the problems are. See if it's your niche.

---

### Insider's Tip!

Does the neighborhood you're researching have any housing projects? A project can hold back development in an entire area. Conversely, a hospital or university provides a dependable demand for housing, with constant high interest even in soft rental markets.

---

### *Hear*

While you're hanging out in the area, listen to the rhythms of the neighborhood. Do you hear very loud music in the cafés? Classical orchestrations in the trinket shops? Lots of chatter through one window can mean many people sharing one apartment. All these sorts of things provide important information about the character of the locale.

Also, take time to talk to anybody who'll spare you a minute. While I was scouting Brooklyn's Clinton Hill neighborhood, I ran across Pratt Institute's campus there, a well-respected school for architecture, design, and fine arts. I'd never heard of the school at the time, but I wanted to know about it as soon as I realized that the neighborhood was fitting into my niche. I spent some time strolling the campus and hanging out in the cafeteria. Then I decided to sign up for a "prospective students" tour. My guide was currently enrolled as a student.

As she escorted me around the facilities—they were pretty impressive—I peppered her with questions, and I listened closely to what she had to say. I learned, for instance, that Pratt costs $25,000 a year. Well, *that* perked up my ears! Students, at age 18, 19, 20, don't have the money to pay for tuition; their parents generally foot the bill, including their housing bill . . . So I asked, "What housing is available? Where are all the dorms?"

"Well, um, we have a real problem," my guide replied. "We don't have enough dorms."

*Cha-ching. This is my market! Artists who need housing!* One person's challenge is another person's opportunity.

Suddenly I knew where I was going to invest. The simple act of listening to this community insider gave me the key piece of information I needed about the neighborhood.

---

### These Are the People in Your Neighborhood

While you are exploring the neighborhood, it's important to talk to the people who live and work there. Some terrific people to seek out and gather information from include the following:

- The proprietor of the corner grocery
- UPS and FedEx delivery people
- Wait staff at the local diner
- Letter carriers
- The support staff in the chamber of commerce or mayor's office

- Service business employees: people who work at the auto body shop, bank, dry cleaner
- And most important: the old guy sitting in front of the corner deli, or the regular customer in the diner

On another visit to the block where I eventually bought my first property, I showed up one Sunday morning to the sound of beautiful gospel music. That's when I noticed the four churches on the street. That solidified my very strong sense of community in the area. I waited until the end of the service and spoke with the pastor, who proudly informed me that the building across the street had been a hotel with hourly rates, that the church had raised money to purchase it, and that the congregation was currently renovating it to become a community center. This is the sort of dramatic transition to take note of. It indicated to me, the real estate investor, a trend change from "tough neighborhood" to "family-value utopia."

### Two Ears

There's great truth to the maxim, "We have two ears and one mouth so we can listen twice as much as we talk." Ask open-ended questions, and then just continue making eye contact, nodding and smiling when appropriate. You will learn so much more from opening your mind—not your mouth!

## Taste and Smell

Let your nose and your taste buds lead you to a neighborhood's eateries. You've probably heard it said that the kitchen is the heart of a home ... well, kitchens are often the heart of a neighborhood, too. They're the places where people gather, relax, talk, gossip, connect, network, let down their guard, and turn into themselves. Eating is a primal, fundamental need, and how the people in an area have chosen to meet it can offer you a glimpse into their souls.

And, of course, there are the fringe benefits. When I started to invest in Jersey, I spent many days there eating Cuban food. This is, by the way, a tax deduction. Now, what could be better than delicious, deductible Cuban food?

It was productive, too. One day while exploring one neighborhood, I went into a café and, utilizing my really poor Spanish, ordered an espresso. "How much?" I asked.

The waitress replied, "Sixty."

I thought I must've misunderstood her; it had been a while since I'd been to Central America. Could *sixty* mean "six dollars"? Wow. More expensive than Starbucks!

So I asked, "What do you mean, sixty?"

"Sixty cents," she told me.

That simple exchange gave me a profound insight into the market I was dealing with. If the local restaurants charge 60 cents for an espresso—a really good espresso, I might add—it reveals a lot about the kind of people living in the area. While I love a good deal, I knew that this area would not serve my niche. Could it be a future hot market? Maybe. Not wanting any information to go to waste, I made a note to revisit this neighborhood once my real estate business had been developed.

Does your market need the 60-cent coffee from the corner deli, or does it prefer the $4.50 coffee from the stylish coffeehouse? One product—or one attitude about a product—can tell you a whole story about a neighborhood.

## *Feel*

Feel the neighborhood? Sure. Most places have a feel or an attitude. Is it a rough-edged neighborhood with broken streetlights, or a soft, idyllic parkland? Do you find beautiful shady lawns, concrete vestibules, or something in between? What's it feel like to take a walk down the sidewalk on hot summer or cold winter days? For that matter, *are* there sidewalks to take a walk down, or do you have to drive everywhere? All of these aspects contribute to the general feel.

This is the point where the rubber meets the road: You want to immerse yourself in the spot. Get in touch with the people's hopes, needs, values, and dreams. Use your head, your heart, and your hands to get involved. Walk, bike, drive, skate, talk, shop, eat, and drink. Volunteer, if you want to. Does this neighborhood seem like a home for your niche?

---

**Insider's Tip!**

What are the new trends, and the transitions the neighborhood is going through, if any? You can make millions just by finding neighborhoods on the verge of a transition and cashing out at the end of it.

---

◆ ◆ ◆

If you've done your scouting homework and gotten all the right answers—if this neighborhood looks, sounds, tastes, smells, and feels like the match you want—if it makes your investor's heart sing—it's time to find out if it'll make your accountant's heart sing, too. Let's turn to the financial side of your research.

## Playing Both Sides

Everything about Brooklyn's Clinton Hill neighborhood was making my heart sing. It had the nucleus of a lively crew of young, artistic residents whose schedules and values meshed perfectly with actors' needs. It had Pratt Institute, desperate for student housing, as a potential secondary source of young, artistic tenants. It had shops and eateries and just a few quirky little boutiques. It felt good. It felt right. (And I can't tell you how excited I was when, just two months after I purchased that property, an Italian restaurant opened down the block.)

But could my future tenants afford it? Could *I*? I needed to know how much housing Clinton Hill had to offer, and at what price.

So I contacted some real estate brokers in the area and set up some tours of properties. Over and over I heard, "Oh, you can easily get a thousand dollars a month for this rental." Or "Two thousand, no problem, I'm telling you." Or "Listen, the rent roll on this place is a thing of beauty."

**rent roll:** Total of current rent collected.

# The Real Estate Millionaire

It sounded great, but I wanted to see these properties from both sides—not just the investors' perspective these brokers were giving me but also the renter's. That is, both my perspective and that of my future tenants.

Here's where the real estate section of newspapers can actually do you a bit of good—at least as a starting point. I began perusing the rental section of the *Village Voice* (a young, artistic paper my niche often reads). I found some Clinton Hill rentals, I called the phone numbers listed, and I went to look at the apartments—as a prospective *renter*. I wanted to see not only the apartments themselves, but especially the kinds of prospective renters who also showed up—and *how many* people came out to see the place. I found some open houses in the area, too, and I attended them—again, as a potential tenant. While I was there, I took the opportunity to chat with the other guests, who told me specifically what they were hoping to find both in the Clinton Hill neighborhood and in their future homes.

All of this opened up a new perspective on Clinton Hill housing for me. I could see what was *really* out there, what it *really* rented for, and the kind of tenants I could *really* expect to attract.

---

### Insider's Tip!

Take a look at the posted signs you see around the neighborhood. You know, the ones on community bulletin boards in grocery stores and Laundromats, on lampposts, walls, and so forth. Here's where you'll often find information about rental and (especially) sublet opportunities you might not learn about otherwise.

In Clinton Hill, for instance, I saw that a typical sign could read: SUBLET. TWO ROOMMATES. $500/MO. This told me that a typical three-bedroom apartment in the area rented for $1,500 a month.

---

Inside a thousand-dollar-a-month one-bedroom rental, for instance, I found a beautiful, unique space with exposed brick, wood floors, and great add-ons. What a treat in New York! Now, a broker had just shown me a similar-sized building nearby—but this comparable property instead featured carpeted floors, dark lighting, and no unique charm. No way would the apartments in that building rent for a thousand a month, as the broker had insisted. Now, what would have happened if I had taken the broker's words as gospel, decided to buy the building, and used his numbers in my calculations? My numbers would have looked very good, but been very wrong. And ultimately, he would have had me operating at a loss.

### Whose Perspective? Whose Agenda?

It's not that real estate professionals are out to mislead you. Like everyone else, they run the gamut. They can be spectacular, scrupled, conscientious . . . or not. But here's what you need to remember: They have an agenda of their own. They want to make a living. They have a vested interest in you making a purchase—they don't get paid until they close the deal!

---

### Extraordinary Broker versus Average Broker

The average broker will paint you the rosiest possible picture of a neighborhood or property. He wants to close the deal.

The extraordinary broker understands that her client is a return customer—or that her customer will refer friends back to her. The extraordinary broker should operate with integrity and provide great service to you. One of my favorite questions to ask a broker is, "What are the challenges or drawbacks to this property?" Ninety-five percent of the brokers I meet will reply, "Well, there aren't many," and will continue to push the pros of the property. These are not the right brokers for me. My best brokers know exactly what I'm looking for and won't waste my time trying to simply line their own pockets.

---

Even the best of brokers will be crossing their fingers that you see value in what they have to offer you. That's true even if they don't have anything that resembles what you're looking for—which is, of course, a good investment that fulfills your requirements based on what you've determined is your niche. Other brokers simply don't want to take the time to understand what investors are looking for. After they close the deal, chances are they'll never see you again. All of this means that whatever comes out of a broker's mouth, you *must* confirm it by doing your own **due diligence.**

> **due diligence:** The careful consideration of each aspect of a proposed asset purchase.

Good real estate professionals are out there, however, and it's often worth your while to tap into their expertise. Talk to them. "I'm looking for an investment property," you might begin:

"What's the best one you have?"

"Can you show the one you just sold?"

"Why is it a good investment?"

"How long have you been in this neighborhood?"

"Do you own any investment property yourself? Tell me about it."

---

## How to Talk Realtor-ese

When I first began nosing around the real estate industry, I knew nothing at all. So I went to a few chatty brokers in town. I told them I had a few hundred thou to invest (I didn't), and could they show me available investments, please? I didn't take my own car—I rode everywhere in the passenger seat with the brokers.

What came next was tough for me: I had to shut up. I sat and listened quietly while brokers regaled me with stories of great deals, fall-through deals, idiosyncratic sellers, and more. They love talking. They love telling stories. (That's what makes them good at their work!) And every time a broker mentioned a new word or phrase—**ROI**, or **rehab**, or **LTV**—I nodded, smiled vaguely, and made a mental note to check out the meaning later that day by jumping on the Internet.

---

> **ROI:** Return on investment.
>
> **rehab:** Short for rehabilitation—the total renovation to an existing building or property.
>
> **LTV:** Loan to value—the relationship in percentages between the loan given (debt) and the total value of the property.

A week after riding around with brokers, I was hip to a bit of industry lingo, so I began peppering my speech with catchy real estate phrases: rent-controlled, rent-stabilized, walk-through inspection, and more. (The glossary on page 179 will help make you an expert terminologist much more quickly.)

After I'd throw out a word, I could almost see the wheels turning in the mortgage or real estate broker's head: Oh, this guy gets it. He's for real—he has the money to invest. I don't have to edit my language. I can just talk.

That's how I learned what real estate professionals have to teach. And each one gave me a little more. Try it for yourself. Every time you come out of a meeting with a real estate pro, write down a few of the insider terms for yourself. Then, when you get home, look them up. Find out what they mean. Practice using them. The next meeting you have, throw one out: "So," you might say, "what's the ROI on that?" Watch the light go on in the pro's eyes: Whoa, here's a person I can respect! Suddenly the quality of information you're getting is going to go way up.

> **rent control:** Tenant-protection laws that prevent landlords from increasing the rent.
>
> **rent stabilization:** Tenant-protection laws that dictate to the landlord how much to increase the rent each year.
>
> **walk-through inspection:** Literally, a walk through the property for purchase just before the closing.

## Action Points: The Real Estate Notebook

Once you start thinking like an investor, you never really stop. Do you remember in the film *The Matrix*, Neo suddenly sees numbers rather than people on the computer screen? It happens in a moment. Everywhere you go, everything you see and do and read and talk about, there will be a little place in the back of your brain somewhere that's thinking, *Where's the real estate in that?*

Keep track of these ideas. You never know which will bear fruit! I keep a special notebook with me all the time, everywhere I go, where I can record stray investment ideas whenever they occur to me.

Go out right now and buy yourself a notebook. You can use whatever *kind* of notebook you like: a three-ring binder; a spiral-bound book of ruled paper; a file on your laptop or PDA. What's important here is that it's a notebook you can have with you everywhere you go, and that you'll really use it—*everywhere you go*—to record your real estate thoughts, dreams, plans, appointments, musings, progress. Do your math here. Keep track of your schedule. Record your impressions of the neighborhoods you visit. Jot down names and contact info for the people you meet. If it happens in your life and it's about real estate, there should be a record of it in your notebook.

Write REAL ESTATE NOTEBOOK on the cover—or title your computer file that way.

And start using it. You'll discover in a hurry how valuable this notebook is. Not only does it provide a paper trail of your every investment idea and action, but it's also a magnificent sourcebook for inspiration when you need it . . . for phone numbers and addresses when you need those . . . and for learning the self-discipline that's so critical to your success now that you're your own boss. You always need that!

You'll hear me refer to your notebook over and over in the pages that follow. Set it up *now* and write down your first thoughts. Then . . . keep writing.

# 4

# Commitment

## The Obstacle

So far your new career is going pretty well, isn't it? You're getting to know your niche. You're researching your neighborhoods. Everything you're doing is interesting, exciting, challenging. *Problems, schmoblems!* you're thinking. *This is a piece of cake!*

But hold on. You're about to run head-on into the critical obstacle that confronts new real estate investors. This is the point at which most new investors are going to stop and say, *I wish . . . but it isn't for me.* Whatever issues you have that could be keeping you from action are going to rear up and bite you. This is where the millionaires are separated from the wannabes.

To be successful in real estate, you must be committed. Unstoppable.

This idea is so crucial to your success that I'm going to say it again: *To be successful in real estate, you must be committed. Unstoppable.*

And here's another certainty for you to consider: The level of success you attain will be determined by your level of commitment. Sure, you want to learn the numbers and techniques and legal terms around real estate—you *need* to learn all that. But it's not what will make you successful. Only your level of commitment will bring about the big wins. This is something that's true not just in real estate but in all of life. And remember: Real estate is about people, nothing else. Your team, your future tenants, your investors are all going to take note of your dedication—or your lack of it. If you're not the kind of person who demonstrates firm resolve—unstoppability—it's going to show. And who wants to get on a train that can't make it up the hills?

So how committed are you? It's time to find out!

## Inspiration versus Commitment

I've seen it over and over again. Someone I know—a friend, an acquaintance, one of my seminar students—gets revved up about an investment career. She can't wait to get out there and *go for it*. She reads, she learns, she's bursting with inspiration—and then she finally jumps in and takes the first step.

But things don't go the way she'd hoped.

So she stops.

Inspiration is like helium, you see. It rises quickly but has no power to sustain over the long term. It sags. It sinks. It flounders.

You *are* going to get discouraged. Why? Because it's human nature to get discouraged. And because not everything is going to go the way you plan or imagine. But here's the difference between successful people and unsuccessful ones: Unsuccessful people fail once or twice and see themselves as failures. Successful people keep trying and failing and failing and trying; and they see their *failures* as failures, not themselves. A failure is just another lesson.

Here's what's going to happen, guaranteed: You'll put an offer on a home, and it will be declined. Or you'll get stuck with delayed renovations. You'll have a terrible contractor whom you'll have to fire. Or perhaps you'll struggle painfully to raise money in the beginning. Or you'll have issues with tenants. Or the market will change. You'll do very well initially because the market is hot . . . and then you'll wake up one day to see a 15 percent drop in your property value. Or something else will happen. So how do you keep that commitment alive when things don't go the way you want?

You must understand the difference between inspiration and commitment. Don't get me wrong here: Inspiration is great. (That's what led you to pick up this book.) You should read as many books as you can, take courses, go to real estate club meetings, join entrepreneur groups; I'll give you even more ideas a little further along in this chapter. But inspiration has a very short shelf life. To deal with that, I teach my students about a crucial process that will keep commitment alive and vivid. I call it the Five-Year Dream.

# Action Point 1: Design Your Five-Year Dream

The next few months will provide the foundation of your real estate career. (Or you might think of it this way: In the next few months, you'll be pouring the concrete to lay the foundation for your real estate business.) No matter what your first investments may be, real estate is a long-term commitment—even if you're doing flips. You need to see clearly where you're heading. So in this activity, you're going to create a future for yourself to essentially step into. You'll be designing a five-year dream, and you're going to do it from the end point back.

> **flip:** The resale of a property immediately following the purchase.

## Step 1. What Does Your Ideal Future Look Like?

Perhaps, in your ideal future, you'll be working the same job as you are now, but only part-time. Maybe you have summers off and spend them at your beach bungalow. That's not bad. That's one level of commitment. If that's what you want, it's great.

But maybe when you open your eyes into your dream life, you find yourself in a huge home in Aspen, or Carmel, or Key West . . . with a Porsche and a Ferrari parked in the garage. You've just returned from a week in Monaco. You don't work anymore, of course, because you're too busy playing golf and frolicking with your kids. Obviously, that's a different level of commitment.

Put aside all cynicism or laziness. Be as specific as you can about what you *really* want—the authentic, inner you. Your goal can be as big or as small as you choose, as long as it's sincere. Knowing your dream is going to help you design your journey.

Once you have that clear picture, write it down! If you don't, it will disappear and you will be a ship without a destination or a compass.

Relax a moment. Imagine it's five years from now. Tap into your core self—the one who doesn't let today's reality cloud tomorrow's dreams. Paint the picture of your life. Don't limit it to material desires. Mentally go through your entire day, toss what doesn't work for you right now, and focus on what really makes you happy. Then expand on that.

My life includes _____.

My life includes _____.

My life includes _____.

My life includes _____.

My life includes _____.

My life includes _____.

My life includes _____.

My life includes _____.

Now take a look at all the parts of your ideal five-year future and write it down in one or two complete sentences. Focus on what you *do* have, rather than what you don't. ("I am financially free and I report only to myself," for instance, as opposed to, "I don't have a boss.")

My dream is _____

_____

_____

_____.

If you dream of a simpler life—still working, but with more free time and maybe a little vacation home to get away to on occasion—the residual income from real estate can easily help put you on the path toward that, and your journey may not take too much sweat.

But if your dreams are bigger and more ambitious—if you want the extravagant homes, the slick cars, and the fabulous vacations—you have to be truly committed, completely focused, and willing to take high risks. Spending a Saturday surfing the Internet and cruising brokers' Web sites is just not going to cut it.

These are both completely valid goals. One is not better than the other, and there are a million different variations that lie between the two. There are no judgments. Just be truthful with yourself.

### Step 2. How Much Money Do You Need to Achieve Your Dreams?

Here's where you begin to translate your dreams into a specific, real-world plan. It's actually a pretty simple step. Look at your life plan and ask yourself, *How much money do I need to make this happen?* If your dreams aren't too far afield from the life you're currently leading, you may be able to figure this out pretty easily. If your goals differ sharply from your current life, however, you may need to do some research. So find out what it would cost you to own a home in Aspen. Check out the down payment, monthly installments, and insurance costs on your Ferrari. Then come up with a number. Would you need $100,000 in passive income every year? $200,000? More? Make it real, even if it looks outrageous to you.

Five years from now, I will be making $_____ in passive income every year.

> **passive income:** Money you don't have to work for.

### Step 3. How Much Real Estate Do You Need to Make That Much Money?

Now it's time to put to work some of that field research you've started doing. You've been chatting with brokers and looking at buildings that fit with your niche. Consider the bottom line of some of the properties that interest you. What will you **net**? (You'll learn more about how to look at finances for yourself in Chapter 6, "The Numbers." For the purposes of this exercise, you can rely on other people's information. Ultimately, you'll always want to crunch your own numbers.)

> **net return:** The amount of money you take in after all your expenses are paid.

Do the math based on your region. Depending on the area of the country you live in (or want to live in) and your passive income target, you may only need a couple of buildings with 10 rental units each. Or maybe you just need one large, industrial rental. If your goal is larger and the area you live in provides a lower return, you might need more.

If you're focusing on residential apartment buildings, you can look at it from the perspective of rental units. In other words, suppose you determine that you'll need one to two hundred units that each net $500 to reach your goals. That might mean 1 or 2 buildings with a hundred units each; 10 to 20 buildings with 10 units each; and so on. It's all about what fits your niche.

Five years from now, I will have _____ buildings that each provide $_____ in passive income per year in my real estate portfolio.

## Step 4. What Route Do You Need to Take to Reach Your Dream? How Are You Going to Get There?

If you've ever taken a long roadtrip, you've probably carefully planned your journey. As you travel, you take careful note of the landmarks along the way. (*Aha! We're in Albany. Time to take a left turn!* Or: *Oh, look. Only 10 more miles to Savannah!*) These landmarks serve not only to tell you that you're on the right path but also to spur you on toward your goal. Within your five-year picture, then, let's create some milestones. When do you want to buy your first property? When will you do your first deal? When will you do your second? And so on.

Let's place your personal pot of gold—the financial freedom you just visualized for yourself—in the heart of a maze we'll call REAL ESTATE. You can begin by entering the maze from the outside, taking wrong turns, backtracking, and wasting a lot of time. Or you can start from that pot of gold, and then move backward toward your starting point. The way out will be surprisingly clearer.

Visualize the road you need to take to reach your dream. Do this by breaking down the larger goal into chunks. And consider your personal working style: Are you a slow starter who gains momentum as you go along? Are you fast out of the gate? Or are you the slow and steady type? Plan appropriately.

Start from your five-year goal in Step 3. Then simply work backward. These are your milestones.

Five years from now, I will have _____ buildings that each provide
$_____ in passive income per year in my real estate portfolio.
Four years from now, I will have _____ buildings that each provide
$_____ in passive income per year in my real estate portfolio.
Three years from now, I will have _____ buildings that each provide
$_____ in passive income per year in my real estate portfolio.
Two years from now, I will have _____ buildings that each provide
$_____ in passive income per year in my real estate portfolio.
One year from now, I will have _____ buildings that each provide
$_____ in passive income per year in my real estate portfolio.

### Step 5. What Are the Hundred Steps You Must Take to Get from One Milestone to the Next?

Okay, I'll concede that you don't need exactly 100 steps between each mile-stone. But know this: The more detailed and broken up the steps are, the easier it will be for you to follow up on them—and to correct yourself when you've chosen the wrong path. It's easy to get overwhelmed when facing a huge task or challenge—I'm sure you know that already. If you simply have a list of things to do, though, the task becomes manageable. You just do it. One step at a time. Even climbing Mount Everest *always* starts with one small step!

Here's how one of my students, a 35-year-old paralegal named Brian, com-pleted this exercise. He summed up his five-year dream for himself like this:

Step 1. My dream is to be able to provide a comfortable life for my par-ents, to spend a month every year traveling, and to create beautiful shared public spaces in my community.

This was a good goal: concrete, clear, and it fit his deepest needs. Then he turned to Step 2, asking himself: *How much money do I need to achieve my dreams?*

This required some research, so Brian broke down his dream into parts, with specific price tags: *How much will buying a residence for my parents cost me? How much do I need to make to be able take a month off? To pay for my travel expenses? How much would it cost me to create shared public spaces? Because these are public spaces, could I get money from public sources?*

He did his homework, found the numbers, and came up with an answer:

Step 2. Five years from now, I will be making $100,000 in passive income every year.

One of the great things about Brian's overall goal was that there was already a lot of real estate in it. Just by pursuing real estate investment, he was going to have the potential to provide a home for his parents and create public spaces in and on the properties he owns. Many of his goals are built right in to the success of his investment plan. This makes his other ambition—spending a month a year traveling—seem much more manageable.

Still, when Brian stopped and looked at the price tag of his dreams, he was appalled: "Good grief! How can I get all that? It's too much!" So I sat down with him and talked him through Steps 3 and 4, looking at the end goal in terms of real estate and then breaking the process down into milestones.

"Tell me," I said, "how much real estate will you need to make $100,000 in passive money per year?"

Brian had been looking at small apartment buildings. That's what he felt most comfortable with, and that's what best fit with his niche. The average net per year of a unit in each of these buildings was $1,000. So he and I did the math: 10 buildings. 10 units each. $1,000 per unit.

Step 3. Five years from now, I will have 10 buildings that each provide $10,000 in passive income per year in my real estate portfolio.

I continued. "Now we break it down. If this is your five-year goal, let's work backward. You need 10 buildings, but you don't need them right now. You need them *in the fifth year* of your plan. So in the fourth year, you'll need seven."

Brian still looked stricken, so I hastened to add, "Hey, it's your fourth year. You're an old pro at this by your fourth year, right?"

Hint of a smile. I could tell Brian would probably be the kind of person who started slow and then picked up speed. With this in mind, I went on, "In your third year, you'll need four buildings. This means that in your second year, you'll need two, and in your first year all you need is one building.

"Think about it. One year from now, you need to own one building. Isn't that easier and more tangible than thinking about a hundred grand?"

So Brian's Step 4 read like this:

Five years from now, I will have 10 buildings that each provides $10,000 in passive income per year in my real estate portfolio.

Four years from now, I will have seven buildings that each provides $10,000 in passive income per year in my real estate portfolio.

Three years from now, I will have four buildings that each provides $10,000 in passive income per year in my real estate portfolio.

Two years from now, I will have two buildings that each provides $10,000 in passive income per year in my real estate portfolio.

One year from now, I will have one building that each provides $10,000 in passive income per year in my real estate portfolio.

By now Brian was grinning and even starting to get excited. So we went on to Step 5, breaking things down even further, step by step. He didn't yet have enough information to plot out every step along his way toward purchasing his first building (see the following chapters to learn this yourself), but he was firmly on the right track. He knew what to do *today* in order to reach his dream in five years. As you break down your dreams into action points like this, you'll find that the insurmountable goals become baby steps.

And one more important point: Don't be rigid in your goals and plan. You're setting up a map to guide you into the future, but if you find a better route, take it. It's all a learning process, and part of that process could be changing your mind. Be flexible with yourself, because a lot can happen over five years' time.

---

### Write It Down

You've heard this one before, but it's worth repeating: As you do this exercise—as you do all the exercises in this book, and even as you think and read and muse about real estate—*write it down*. If you don't, your dreams will slide right off your radar.

It is so easy to get discouraged and say, "Real estate is not for me. It's [*insert Excuse A here*]. I'm [*insert Excuse B here*].

There's [*insert Excuse C here*]." Those are the moments when you need to open up your notebook and remind yourself what it's all for. Have a record. When something is written down, it takes on a reality it just doesn't have in your head.

I keep my road map—my Five-Year Dream—hanging on my office wall. It's front and center in my space, so it's front and center in my professional life as well.

## More about Commitment

When I put together my own five-year picture, one of the things I committed to was considering 45 deals before deciding whether real estate was for me. This was one of my hundred steps, a critical one. I wrote it down. I announced it to my friends and family. I made a point of it to my father. I meant it.

When I started out in 2000, New York City—indeed, the whole of the country—was still in the midst of the high-tech, dot-com boom. (Also known as *the good old days*. I'm sure you remember them.) Many of the folks who were riding that wave were pouring their cash into cool houses in neighborhoods that I was looking at for investment—which meant I had lots of competitors, and many of them were all-cash buyers.

By the time I'd reviewed 30 deals, I'd worked myself into a state of exhaustion—and I *still* couldn't find anything that was right for me. Every property I saw came with a prohibitive price tag; it was clear that if I bought it, I would be challenged to even cover my expenses.

I was hard up against that brick wall I mentioned at the beginning of this chapter. One that was maybe a hundred feet thick. So I called my dad. "I can't find a single deal that makes sense," I moaned. "I guess I don't have it. Real estate's not for me."

Dad made it clear that he understood and empathized and was there for me . . . and did not want to hear one more word of it. "Just go look at your notebook," he said. So I did. There, of course, was my very first commitment, printed bold as brass: ASSESS 45 DEALS. So on I went. And the 32nd property I looked at became my first deal. After 14 months, I sold that property for a net profit of just over $360,000.

## Commitment

Here are some questions to ask yourself to get clear about your commitment:

- **Why am I doing this?** For the average person, it doesn't make sense to take risks. So what is it that makes the risks of a real estate career worthwhile for you? The challenge? The potential for financial independence? The chance to be your own boss? Know your reasons—your real, deep-down, soul reasons—and you'll always know how to motivate yourself when a little spark is needed.
- **What am I willing to give up?** I used to wake up at 8 A.M. on Saturday and Sunday to look at property (and remember, I was an actor—8 A.M. was the middle of the night). What are *you* willing to give up to create this new business for yourself? Time? Money? Sleep? Social life? The level of sacrifices you're prepared to make is a good way to measure your level of commitment. And let me remind you of something I said at the beginning of this chapter: *The level of success you attain will be determined by your level of commitment.*
- **What am I going to do when I'm rich?** Once I got started in this field, I fell in love with real estate. I walked New York's streets admiring the beauty of the architecture; I got excited about going to Home Depot; I skipped meals to pore over spreadsheets. I chose to love every aspect of this business. That's a big part of why I do this. But it's not all.

I do this work to give my children a secure future. And I do it to give back to my community. And—okay, okay—I do it to get my hands on a few cool new toys. I do this for the money. You will, too. What will you do with it? What deep-down soul-satisfying things will you do once you're rich? The answers lie in the question *How much is enough for me?* If you had $10 million or $50 million, what would you do? I'm talking *beyond* securing a future for your children. That *thing* you identify, whatever it is . . . that's the reason you want to do this.

# Moving beyond Knowledge

There are thousands of diet books on the market, yet people still don't lose weight. This is because it's not enough *just to know how* to lose weight. The same principle applies to real estate.

The next few chapters of this book are all about knowledge. You're going to read all about the money, the numbers, the legalities, the logistics. It's important stuff—yet before you read even a single word of it, you need to move *beyond* it and focus instead on what will get and keep you committed.

Let's get you going with some juicy sources of support to get you keyed in to your new life! (By the way, the secret to losing weight is to eat less, move more. That's it.)

# 1. Finding the Spark of Inspiration: A Resource List

Inspiration is not the same thing as commitment, but it sure does have its place. It won't create a long-term career for you, true, but sometimes all you need is something to get you up off your butt and out the door and working on your tasks for *today*.

What inspires me? I've learned that my own best sparks come from going to open houses; seeing a building in the middle of construction on in; before-and-after pictures. So I keep photos of my properties on my screen saver as a constant reminder of what I'm doing all of this *for*.

As you continue in your real estate journey, you'll discover your own fire starters and flame keepers—the ones that work for you. Make a list. Every time you see something that inspires you, write it down. Heard about a great course someone took? Write it down. Saw a great book about how to manage your own business? Write it down. Keep your list active, and keep it always at hand. Commit yourself to exploring every source you've listed— a book each month, a Web site each week, whatever you need. Now, whenever you need to light a fire under your rear end, you know exactly how.

## Seminars

Attending real estate seminars and classes is a wonderful way to recharge your batteries and redouble your commitment. I can always find things I don't already know at these events. Even if I already "know" everything that's being presented (or think I do), they still offer me an opportunity to hear concepts and ideas in new and different ways, which helps them truly sink in.

It's very powerful to be surrounded by people who all share the same basic goal: bettering their lives. And just think about the networking possibilities! After all, the individuals who go out and attend seminars are already motivated. They could turn out to be terrific business partners for your real estate pursuits.

You can find some great entry-level seminars—both real-estate-related and others—offered by the following folks:

- **Landmark Education** (www.landmarkeducation.com) offers a weekend seminar called the Landmark Forum, which gives you the tools to break through your fears and focus on your commitments.
- T. Harv Eker's **Millionaire Mind** (www.peakpotentials.com) is also a weekend seminar (usually free of charge, or pretty close to it) that challenges your notions of wealth and encourages you to open up your life to include wealth and abundance.

---

### Seminar Caution #1

Always remember that the people who put on seminars are in a profit-making business themselves. Part of the agenda for a weekend seminar may well be persuading you to buy the next seminar—and the next one . . .

---

- **Rich Dad, Poor Dad** (www.richdad.com). Robert Kiyosaki became famous with his series of *Rich Dad, Poor Dad* books and parlayed them into an empire of seminars, companion CDs, and even board games. He offers basic information in a very inspiring, *you-can-do-this* fashion.
- **Robert Allen's** real estate course (http://multiplestreamsofincome.com) inundates you with information: an eight-CD set; a gargantuan binder filled with forms, rules, and information; and a mentoring program.

---

### Seminar Caution #2

At my own *Real Estate Millionaire* seminars, I frequently run across what I call "seminar junkies"—those individuals who attend class after class, weekend after weekend, and never quite seem to get into the action of making real estate acquisitions. "Oh, I just need this one more piece of information on tax liens that's being offered for $4,000 dollars next weekend!" I've heard. Or, "Next month I'll learn about rehabs. Then I can start buying."

If you were to pool all the money these people have spent attending seminars—well, they could've bought their own property by now without even finding investors!

---

## Books

- Robert Allen and Mark Victor Hansen's *The One-Minute Millionaire* perfectly reflects the spirit of generosity, team, and fun that's present in business building at its finest. I give *The One-Minute Millionaire* to my new employees and to potential business partners; it puts us on the same page from day one. The book is written as both a fiction story (on the right-hand pages) and as nonfiction (left-hand pages). I recommend you read the fiction story first.

- Within the *Rich Dad, Poor Dad* library, you'll find *Real Estate Riches*, by Dolf de Roos. This is a tiny, simple book that lays out the benefits of real estate ownership. If you're reading this, you've already graduated beyond de Roos's information, but it's still a good book to recharge your batteries—and to give to someone who doesn't know anything about real estate ownership.

- Michael Gerber's *The E-Myth* and *The E-Myth Revisited* teach you how to take your business from the "technician" stage (you're doing everything yourself, hands-on), to the "manager" stage (people are working for and with you—but if you leave, the place crumbles), to the "mogul" stage (the business runs with or without you, and you have created ongoing residual income for yourself—bravo!). Gerber lays all this out with many *aha!* moments for the business owner and not-yet-business-owner alike.

---

**More Sparks**

Still looking for motivation? Here are some more ideas:
- I constantly read newspapers' real estate sections—as a source of *inspiration* rather than knowledge.
- I ask people how much they paid for their homes. (At first, yes, I found this a little uncomfortable. Then I got over it.)
- I subscribe to magazines. Try **Entrepreneur** magazine, for a start.
- Cable TV offers myriad programs on the real estate market.
- Listen to audiotapes on real estate investing, on business building, on life changing, and so forth.
- Go to Borders, pick out a few books from the real estate section, get yourself a big cozy cup of coffee, and settle in.

---

### *The Internet*

The only hard part about using the Internet for inspiration is getting *off* the Internet and into action! The last few years have been an intensive immersion course in World Wide Web Studies for everyone, especially real estate investors. You'll find some of my own favorite Web sites peppered throughout this book, and you'll find more, lots more, on your own.

If the Web is your thing, spend time there. Once a week, surf the Net looking only at real estate. Another great Web tool for many folks is chat rooms—look around for investment-oriented sites that are positive, upbeat, inspiring.

## 2. Putting Yourself Out There: How to Start Talking and Whom to Talk to

Once again, it's time to pull out your real estate notebook (notice how indispensable it's becoming to you?) and a pen. Now drag over your Rolodex or PDA and go at it: Who's in there who might know a whit about real estate? Do you have a distant cousin who owns some land in Oklahoma? Is there a friend-of-a-friend who likes investing in REITs? Call around. Put out the word that you are focusing your efforts on real estate investing and would be thrilled to talk to anyone with some free advice to give. You'll note how happy people are to share their experiences with you, too. Give folks the chance to be experts and they will happily oblige you, possibly for hours at a time.

> **REIT (real estate investment trust):** A publicly traded company that invests in real estate.

If all of this is starting to sound a little intimidating—if this kind of conversation is outside your comfort zone—that's okay. You can deal with it. Think of it as a big game, which it is. (Did I mention yet how much *fun* real estate can be?) But it's a game that starts with tiny little steps. Remember the milestones you created as part of your Five-Year Dream, and the hundred steps between each milestone? In this business, you measure yourself with tiny little steps. That's what it's all about.

Here are a few things to try out:

- Have two conversations this week that include the words *real estate*. Even if they're with friends, they still count—you never know who just inherited money, or who's dying to dump a property.
- Practice introducing yourself as a real estate investor. (You don't need a degree to be a real estate investor. It's not like you're declaring yourself a surgeon, or a police officer.) If this sounds silly, be assured that it's not. There's a ripple effect to these things. Eventually—it won't take long—people are going to know that you're a real estate investor. It'll just be part of your identity, of who you are. And you'll think of yourself that way, too!
- Get yourself some business cards and hand out two a day for a week. The next week, bump it up to three a day. Keep on challenging yourself. Pretty soon it all becomes easy.

Who to talk to? Well, *everyone*. Still, here are a couple of pointers—some ways to talk to people that can really get your career off the ground:

First, create a network of like-minded souls—folks just as much on fire about real estate investing as you are. When I got started, I belonged to an informal group set up with eight other people from different professions. We got together and brainstormed challenges and inspirations around our various fields of expertise. I owe a lot of my inspiration and success of my business to this team.

Just as important, spend time with, and be influenced by, individuals who are more advanced than you are—those who've already "made it." If you know them personally, ask them out for coffee. If you don't, try offering yourself as an assistant or apprentice.

> *I met a woman named Kim in a seminar we both took. She followed up with me with several e-mails, and then she called to set up a lunch meeting. I was too busy. She sent me a few more e-mails. Finally she just showed up one day in my seminar! "I need to work for you—I'll do it for free," she said.*
>
> *What made me take Kim on as an apprentice? She was committed, and she didn't take no for an answer. She spent a few months in my office, she was an enormous help to me, and she learned a lot. Now she's out on her own and doing very well indeed.*

# 3. Allocating Time: The Effort versus Success Model

Momentum is a powerful force. For every one unit of result, you must first put in 100 units of effort. Give it time, though, and things will flip—you'll achieve a hundred units of success for a single unit of effort.

*But you're not there yet.* In the beginning, you will get discouraged. (Remember my hundred-foot-thick brick wall?) You'll be convinced that your goal is unreachable, the wall is insurmountable, the whole world just *stinks* and you might as well slink back to your day job. So you read this chapter . . . you reread your real estate notebook . . . you revisit some of your best inspiration sources . . . in short, you keep plugging away. You do this because you're committed. The whole world still stinks, but it stinks while you're doing your real estate homework.

Remember when you first learned how to read? In the beginning, it was letter by painstaking letter. Now your eyes fly over the page.

In the beginning of my investment career, I had to run around like crazy looking at deals. I put out a *lot* of effort, and yes, much of it was an utter waste of time, because I didn't know where to look or what questions to ask. (Lucky you, you have this book. You'll know all the questions ahead of time—and the answers, too.) Now, however, deals come to me. I no longer have to be the one putting out the feelers—people know what I'm up to, and they come to me.

It's the law of momentum. Keep plugging away and eventually, ultimately, for every unit of effort you expend, you'll get back a hundred units of reward.

Think of a rock sitting on the top of a hill. It's a big rock; a heavy one. It's hard to move. And it'll sit there at the top of the hill for a long, long time. Get it started, though—actually put in the effort to nudge that rock, even just an inch—and it'll start to roll. Slowly, at first, but then faster and faster.

That's momentum. Your real estate career is like that. When all you're doing is dreaming about it, it's just sitting on the top of the hill. All the inspiration in the world won't move that rock.

What will is effort. Get out and do something. Take an action. Move the rock. And just *see* what happens then!

### Set Yourself Concrete Mini Goals

Go back to your Five-Year Dream and take a look at the milestones you set for yourself. Then look at the hundred (or so) steps you created to reach each milestone. There's your to-do list, sitting right in front of you. Each entry is simple, manageable, doable.

### Schedule Your Mini Goals

Your momentum can be directly correlated to your schedule. If you really want to make it, *but you don't schedule it*, real estate investment becomes just one more thing on your to-do list that never happens.

From now on you need to schedule real estate investment time directly into your calendar. (See the Action Points at the end of this chapter.) This time will be dedicated *only* to fieldwork in real estate. This is different from the inspiration work we talked about earlier—this is the nuts-and-bolts, what's-for-sale, when-can-I-see-it, let-me-give-you-my-offer work. And you must treat this appointment with yourself like it's an appointment with your boss. (Which, if you think about it, it *is*.)

If you put it in your schedule but make excuses when it arrives ("Yes, but I have to do laundry." "Yes, but I have to go to the gym."), it will slide right off your radar screen and out of existence—and along with it will go that million dollars you're dreaming about.

### Create Systems That Keep You Accountable for Your Mini Goals

Every week, schedule a one-hour review session. Go over the goals you had for the week that just ended. Did you achieve all of them? How well? Do you need to continue working on them in the coming week? What new goals will you set for yourself this week? Revise your calendar for the days ahead, adding your new goals and your continuing work as needed.

If you can, hold group review sessions. Seek out or create a network of fellow investors who meet regularly to review each other's progress and hold each other accountable for it. This regular group meeting could take place in person, on the phone, on the Internet—doesn't matter. It might involve 2 people or 20—that doesn't matter either. What matters is doing it. And you'll be amazed at everything a group of peers has to offer you—reviewing, advising, nagging, laughing, deploring, cheering, and in general kicking you out of your chair and into action.

# Action Point 2: The Real Estate Calendar

Get yourself a month-by-month calendar—one of those beautiful wall-mounted versions, or a desk-blotter type, or a computer program; the format doesn't matter. Whatever calendar you use, sit down right now and enter the following items onto it. Then—starting today—complete them!

### Things to Insert on Your Schedule Right Now

- Read a real estate book (every month).
- Spend an hour surfing real estate Web sites (every week).
- See two properties (every weekend).
- Attend a real estate seminar (every quarter).
- Go back to the Five-Year Dream you constructed earlier in this chapter. Review Concrete Mini Goal #1 (Week 1).

- Review Concrete Mini Goal #2 (Week 2).
- Review Concrete Mini Goal #3 (Week 3).
- Review Concrete wMini Goal #4 (Week 4).
- Review progress on my Mini Goals (every week).
- Have two real estate conversations (every day).
- Hand out two business cards (every day).

# 5

# Cold Hard Cash

Most people are convinced they need a lot of money in order to invest in real estate. But what if you don't have a wad of cash lying around? How do you go about starting in real estate without any money? One of the biggest obstacles you'll face is the belief—and it's *just* a belief—that you need a lot of money to invest in real estate. This is, to put it plainly, BS. It is true that real estate needs a lot of money—I agree with that. *Raising* the money, however, can be simple. You use your assets—but *not* your money.

Let's talk about how you can shift your perspectives on money and become creative.

## Capital Source #1: Home, Sweet Home Equity

How to raise **capital**? There are many, many sources of money. First on the list is your own property. Now, don't skip this section if you don't own anything yet—I am quite sure you know someone who owns some kind of real estate. So go ahead and read through everything that follows, keeping people that you know in mind, because soon you'll be sharing your real estate adventure—and all its benefits—with them.

> **capital:** Money!

If you do own property yourself, you may have megabucks tied up in it. Maybe it's a lot of money, period; maybe it's a lot for *you*. Either way, though, it's money that isn't being used. If you want to invest in real estate, you need to pull this money out of your property, and you do so via a mortgage or home equity loan.

Suppose you bought yourself a small home a while back—it was all you could afford. Then suddenly the real estate market got hot, and the value of your house went through the roof. Well, you can now go to the bank and say, "Lend me some money against my home." Most banks would be delighted to do just that.

It's a great way to start. It's why you don't need a lot of money to launch yourself into real estate: Banks will lend you a lot of money.

What you *do* need to get this process rolling—and I'm talking in broad, sweeping terms here—is a percentage of the loan you're seeking. Here are a couple of general rules:

- If you're seeking a residential mortgage—a loan to finance a property of up to about five units—you'll need to put up about 10 percent of the total yourself.
- If you're seeking a mortgage for any other type of property—a retail unit, a **mixed-use**, a 700-unit high-rise, what have you—you'll need to put up about 25 percent of the total.

> **mixed-use:** Residential and commercial units in the same building.

Your particular situation and lender may require more than this, or the total may be less. Still, these are realistic starting points to work from.

If you have $100,000, then, you can buy a property that runs close to $1 million—which is a lot of money for a property. *You don't need to raise that $1 million*—you only need to raise $100,000. Or, if you have an extra $60K from an apartment you used to own, you can use that to finance a really great first investment for half a million.

How does this actually work? Let's return to that little house you bought awhile back. We'll say you bought it six years ago, for $400,000. At that point you put 20 percent down, or $80,000, and got a $320,000 mortgage. (You didn't know the power of leverage back then, which explains the "20 percent" figure.) You got 80 percent LTV—loan to value.

Equity
20%

Mortgage
80%

**Figure 5.1.** Home chart.

> **LTV:** Loan to value—the relationship in percentages between the loan given (debt) and the total value of the property.

Six years have passed, and you know from watching a few neighbors sell their houses that yours is now worth, conservatively, $600K. So here's what you do: You go to the lenders at the bank and tell them, "I'd like to refinance my house." This time, however, you're only going to put 10 percent down. You don't have to come up with the full 20 percent of the money—it's already in your house, in the form of equity. So you say to the bank, "I'd like a 90 percent mortgage." (This can be any bank, by the way—whichever gives you the best rate.) The bank will send an appraiser to your home to confirm that it is indeed worth what you think it is. And even with bad credit, if you've got a property like this worth $600K to use as collateral, you can find a bank that will give you a 90 percent mortgage—$540,000.

At the closing of the refi, the bank will pay off the old mortgage. This started at $320,000, as you'll recall, and you've now paid it down to about $310,000. (Take a look at the upcoming sidebar for the details on how this works.) Once the $310K is disbursed, you're left with $230K to invest.

**refi:** Real-estate-speak for "refinance."

Read that again: two hundred and thirty thousand dollars. This is a tremendous amount of money to start with!

## Math Break

Let's pause for a second and understand why the balance of your mortgage reduced by only $10,000 in six years.

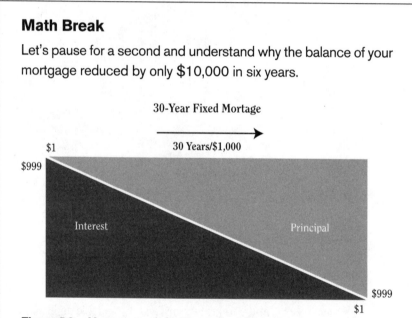

**Figure 5.2.** Mortgage graph for 30-year fixed mortgage.

The bank considers mortgages a long-term investment. So it wants to make sure that if you pay off all the money before the expected time frame, it still makes a profit. Indeed, the bank wants to make a profit from the first *day*. (Heck, wouldn't you?)

This is how your bank will set up the contract, then (and it's a simplified version, but the basic concepts are here): It gives you

> a 30-year fixed mortgage that requires you to pay $1,000 a month. In the first month, the contract calls for $1 of your payment to be applied to the loan principal, but $999 to its interest. Thirty years from now, however, the last payment you'll make on this mortgage will be $999 principal, and $1 interest.

At this point, some of you are saying to me, "Sure, but now I've got a huge mortgage on my house. *Now* what?" Well, if you take your $230,000 and go spend it on a new yacht, that's a real concern. If, however, you invest the money straightaway into real estate, you'll be making enough in passive income to cover any increase in your monthly mortgage payments.

### Insider's Tip!

If you refinance during a low-interest-rate market, there's a chance that your new mortgage payments won't be any higher than your original mortgage payments. Hard to believe, but true! In a low market, you may well be able to lock in a lower interest rate, thus offsetting the hike in principal payments.

### *Buried Treasure*

What if the day after you bought your house you began a few small renovations. And there underneath the basement flooring, you found a treasure chest filled with gold coins—worth hundreds of thousands of dollars. This would make the front page of the local paper, no doubt—and it'd make your day, too.

Well, the reality is that *everyone* who owns a home for more than five years has just such a treasure available . . . they simply don't know where to find it. But now you do: It's called home equity.

I love using the home equity approach to finance your real estate kingdom. Why? Perhaps the best part is that it uses money that was just lying there, right in your house. It's money you weren't planning on saving—you didn't have to tighten your belt, didn't have to open a savings account or mutual fund, did not, in fact, have to do one thing.

Why else do I love it? You're using the cheapest money available. *And you leverage what is already leveraged*. This is called **compounding**. According to a popular legend, Albert Einstein once called compound interest "the most brilliant mathematical concept of all time." Whether he really said this is still being debated—but if he didn't, he should've. It is.

> **compounding:** The process of reinvesting interest to earn additional interest. The more frequent the compounding, the more you earn. Compounded interest is paid on both the accumulated interest as well as the original principal.

Why else? You don't have to find partners—investors—who will be expecting aggressive returns on their investment. And nearly any bank will be delighted to give you a 90 percent mortgage—no matter your credit.

So what could go wrong? Well . . .

- At the closing of the refinance, you will get a check for $230,000. And I've seen way too many of my friends and seminar students who suddenly found the new SUV at the corner Lexus dealership looking awfully tempting—even logical. (*C'mon, look at all the money I have! What's $40K? I'll have plenty left over for real estate . . .*) Then a quick vacation looks good, too. (*I've still got $190K left, right?*) Then pretty soon all you're left holding is a heftier mortgage from your refi, and lots of liabilities.

    *Don't do this.*

- I've seen a lot of other folks who are so terrified at the prospect of increasing their liabilities, they won't even consider refinancing a mortgage. *Wrench this fear from your life—now and forever*. Your house is simply a tool for you to make money. It is not your piggy bank. Only lower- and middle-class people see their homes as investments. The wealthy know how to leverage every source they have to reach their goals and get what they want.

Of course, if you make $10 million and you want to feel comfortable, go ahead and pay off your mortgage. Right now, however, while you're struggling to even pay your bills, is the time you need to leverage.

## The American Dream?

My parents' generation—the boomers—were indoctrinated with the ideals of owning a home. My wife's parents had a party when their 30-year mortgage was paid off. They had achieved the American Dream. They owned a home!

Well, not really. You actually don't own your real estate. You may live there, if it's your primary residence. You may have the illusion—and we dearly want to have this illusion—that you actually own it. But you don't. Even if you've paid your mortgage in full, every red cent—you still don't own this property. Because if you don't pay the city taxes, the city's going to take it. If you don't pay the federal taxes, the state's going to take it. The government, I assure you, will be happy to procure your home.

You never really own any real estate; someone else always has the power to take it away from you. So stop being attached to the idea that a house is "yours." It's not. If you want to get attached to something, get attached to the image of being worth $20 million—and enjoying a lifestyle to match!

### A Home Equity Alternative: HELOC

Let's go back to our homeowning scenario: You bought a house six years ago for $400,000, putting down 20 percent, with a mortgage of $320,000. The house is now worth $600K; your mortgage, $310K.

This time, however, instead of refinancing, you're going to apply for a HELOC.

**home equity line of credit (HELOC):** A mortgage on your home that operates like revolving credit. You may borrow none, a portion, or all of the available credit based on your needs.

The process is very similar. You'll go to a bank and show the lenders there that you do indeed have equity in your home. When you get your money this time, however, you won't use it to pay off your current mortgage; instead, the bank will add revolving credit on top of that mortgage. Think of it as a sort of revolving door: Money comes in, money goes out, as frequently and as much as you need or want.

At the closing of your HELOC loan, you won't get a check for $230K. What you'll get instead is a checkbook that gives you the option of writing a check as large as $230K (and sometimes as small as $200).

So what's the difference between a refi and a HELOC—and why do I vote for the HELOC?

**Reason 1.** What if it takes you four months or six months to find your first great deal? If that turns out to be the case for you, with a HELOC you won't be touching your money until you need it—which means you won't be paying interest on that money during all those months you don't use it. With the HELOC's open checkbook, you wait until the closing of the new real estate deal and *only then* begin paying interest.

**Reason 2.** What if you find a great real estate deal that requires an investment of only $100K? With a HELOC, you'll pull those funds from your line of credit—and you'll pay interest *only* on the $100K. You won't be paying interest on the full $230,000.

**Reason 3.** If you find a great deal that you need to close on quickly, it is—trust me—very impressive if you can write a check for $100K on the spot. This can be a terrific tool for negotiation.

**Reason 4.** Banks charge much lower closing costs for a HELOC than they do for a refi—sometimes *no* closing costs. This can be a substantial savings, because closing costs on a mortgage might run as high as 5 percent of the loan. (These costs include title insurance, mortgage insurance, mortgage taxes, professional fees, and more. Chapter 7, "Close the Deal," details each of these expenses.)

---

### Insider's Tip!

During low-interest-rate markets, a HELOC will be cheaper than a mortgage.

---

So what could go wrong? Well . . .

- Walk into your bank's local branch office to get a HELOC and you'll likely spot promotional posters full of people waterskiing, or smiling away in their new kitchens. Banks want you to spend this money not on real estate investment, you see, but on unnecessary liabilities—exactly the same strategy that credit card companies employ. You're smarter than this. Keep your Five-Year Dream firmly in mind.

---

## Teaser Rates

There is one case in which you might want to take a bank up on its promise of fast money. It's called the teaser rate. Many banks will encourage you to spend money on the very first day you receive your HELOC by promising you a lower rate–even up to 1 percent lower–for pulling out $20,000 or $30,000 at the closing.

If you do get this offer, here's my recommendation: Go ahead and take out $20,000 at the closing–then return it within a few days. If you'll be charged 5 percent interest (for example) on that $20,000, this means you'll be paying $2.74 per day. In return, you'll be locking in a terrific interest rate–and the whole gambit is completely legal.

Check with your mortgage broker to discover the minimum time–if any–that the bank requires you to leave the money out. In most of the cases I've seen, there is no minimum time frame–which means you could replace that money in one day. Be sure to read the fine print, however, or have your mortgage broker read it with you!

---

- The interest rate on a HELOC is never fixed. As this rate goes up, the cost of your monthly payments will, of course, go up right along with it. How to avoid this? Use the HELOC as a bridge until you close on the investment property that your HELOC is intended for. Then turn around and refinance your original house by paying off the HELOC and locking in the mortgage.

# Capital Source #2: All You People, Come Together

The next source of capital on your list is other people.

When you read the preceding section on home equity—on using the value of the property you already own—you may have said, "But I don't own property." Sound familiar? Well, listen up: When I refer to "your property," I'm really referring to the property of anyone you have ever met.

All kinds of people you know own property. And I'm not talking here just about your Rich Old Uncle Wally who can sit down and write you out a check for $2 million. (Not that there's anything wrong with that . . .) Nope, I'm talking about your cousin Cathy, the frantically busy attorney, who has that $50 grand she's managed to put aside—and would love to go into a venture with you. Why? Because she has plenty of money (okay, a bit of money), and she has zero time to spend investing it.

I'm talking about Mom and Dad, who own their house outright but are already in their early sixties. If they want to retire comfortably, they're going to need some passive income, and they know it.

I'm talking about Bill, your high school buddy, who has $30,000. And Ned, your neighbor, with $20K. All these people—family, extended family, family extended out to encompass everyone you know. When you put them all together, suddenly you have $100,000. And guess what? That's enough money to start with.

Sure, it'd be great to go into real estate investment all on your own—and if you can, good for you! There's nothing better or more satisfying. Most of us, however, don't have six figures lying around. That's why you need to start talking.

Don't ever say that you don't know anyone with money. It's just not true. For most of us, our most important real estate asset is a big mouth. If you don't have one, get one!

*Scott, a student at one of my real estate seminars, complained to me that he had no assets and no network—he'd just moved to New York City, where he was working as a waiter, far from his family, trying to make it in the theater. I encouraged him to start introducing himself to people as a real estate investor—whether he felt like one or not, and even if he was convinced he didn't know anyone with cash. He agreed to give it a try. He didn't have much to lose!*

*And then one night at work, Scott got to talking with a fellow waiter, Grant. Turned out that Grant was trying to figure out what to do with $40,000 he'd just inherited from his grandparents. Scott and Grant partnered on their first deal.*

You never know. So talk. Talk to friends and family and neighbors. Talk to coworkers. Talk to folks in line at the coffee shop and the movie house. Talk!

Put all these folks together, and there you have it: your investment group.

### The Limited Liability Company

The limited liability company (LLC) is a very simple business structure that the federal government created about 10 years ago. It costs a few hundred dollars to set one up, and you do need to open it in the same state you'll do your business in.

In highly simplified terms, an LLC is a formal, legal way to split shares among a group of investors. You can set it up to meet the specific needs of your investment group, spelling out each member's contributions, responsibilities, returns, and so forth.

It's also a kind of firewall between you and catastrophe. The *limited liability* part of the name here means that if a tenant ever sues you for any reason—say, he fell down the stairs and broke his leg—any damages awarded will come from the corporation, not from you or any of your investors personally. Given our lawsuit-happy culture, this can save you from financial ruin.

I'm not an attorney, and I can't give legal advice, but I've had very good experiences with LLCs—they're easy to understand, easy to set up, and can work well for all their members. You do need a lawyer to help you create one, and she can give you all the details, advice, and paperwork you need. There's also more information online to help you wrap your mind around the concepts and decide if an LLC is right for you. Try www.bizfilings.com, for starters.

---

## The Downside of LLCs

When it comes time to find and sign a mortgage, the LLC structure might limit your options. Banks, you see, are often leery about lending to LLCs—especially newly formed LLCs. They'd rather see their mortgages guaranteed by a *person* than by a corporation. You'll need what's called a **nonrecourse mortgage**. A lot of banks don't like these.

**nonrecourse mortgage:** A mortgage in which the bank agrees to lend to a corporation from the very beginning.

It's tricky to get a nonrecourse mortgage in the beginning—and to be honest, as a fledgling investor it needn't be a priority for you. (After all, you have nothing anyone might want for recourse!). When your assets start adding up, however, this could be a crucial protection for you. Be sure to talk to your lawyer and lender about it.

One final word: Don't even think about buying a property in your own name then transferring it to your LLC. That's a change of ownership, and it's illegal. It gives the bank the right to recall its loan—which means it asks for the entire loan amount back, right away. This is not a possibility you ever want to entertain.

---

## Capital Source #3: Sweat Equity

Now we're talking: Sweat equity is how I began real estate investing.

As the name implies, *sweat equity* means you receive equity—ownership—in exchange for your sweat. So your cousin Cathy, the frantically busy attorney who has money but no time, puts up some funds. Mom and Dad invest their home equity while they rev up the RV for their first retirement adventure. Your buddies and neighbors and coworkers—the members of your investment group—put up their shares of the capital and go back to their day jobs. And you, who has time but no money, put in the sweat: reading this book, learning the basics, finding the properties, closing the deals.

Once you've used your big mouth (see above) to find your investors, you get them together and say, "You know what? We have enough to go in on a deal. Each one of you brings $20,000. I don't have any money. But what I'll do, I'll do all the work for you. I'll find a deal for you. I'll make sure it's happening. And when we buy the place, I'm also going to manage the building. I'm going to make sure the tenants pay rent. I'm going to do everything that needs to be done. That'll be my share."

A lot of people will be delighted with this. You'll meet many, many folks who are eager to invest and put their money to work, but they just do not want to deal with real estate. They're afraid that it's going to be a hassle; they're afraid they don't have the time or interest to deal with the daily nitty-gritty of property owning. So you tell them, "You know what? You just put up the money. I'll do all the real work." And if these people trust you— if they know you to be personable and reliable and honest—they'll jump right in, and there you are: in business.

## All Sweat Is Not Created Equal

It's pretty easy to figure out what proportion of a property its financial investors own: Each share is proportionate to each contribution. But what about you with your labor? How do you know what your sweat is worth? My advice is to start small. Take a small percentage—enough to keep you sustained and no more.

I've said this before and you'll hear me say it a lot more in this book: Be generous. Be generous with your investors—the family and friends and colleagues who give you their money. I can't say this enough.

No matter who you know—and I mean even if Donald Trump is your best racquetball buddy—if you don't have a good name, you won't get anywhere in real estate. Yet as soon as people know you to be honest, responsible, and, yes, generous, they'll come to you. I never spent a dime on any PR work; people just came to me. Even though I didn't have any experience, still, for whatever reason, they trusted me. They gave me a start.

Now, this doesn't mean you've got to be just as generous for the rest of your life. Think long-term. Because as your knowledge grows, and your success grows, you're going to say, "No, actually, I'm going to charge more money now." You'll be worth it, and your investors will know it.

But for the first few deals, just be generous. Your investment group will turn into your agents and backers and promoters. They'll run to their friends to brag of all the money they're making—the money *you're making for them*. When you make mistakes on your early deals—and you will—they'll forgive you. They'll be supportive. They'll be real partners. Why? They respect you.

---

### Insider's Tip!

Allow yourself a learning curve. In this business, you'll need it. Your mistakes are just that—mistakes. They're not reflections on your integrity, your dedication, or your ability.

---

Sweat equity requires moving beyond a tunnel-vision focus on money and the bottom line. Instead, you commit yourself to providing value for your investors. If you put the work in honestly, you will create a universally rewarding situation for your investors and yourself.

## Creative Capital: The Good, the Great, and the Ugly

Up to now we've been talking about more or less traditional real estate transactions: You see a property, you like it, you decide to buy it, you put some money down and get a loan for the rest—*poof!* Deal done. It's how you and yours probably bought all the property you've ever owned.

It's a fine way to do business, but it's not the only one. Below are some more inventive financing options that you may not have considered. Most of them are definitely worth a thought.

### *"No Money Down!"*

Catchy slogan, but in my experience . . . this one *isn't* a reliable method or strategy.

As I see it, the "no-money-down" deal (also known as "zero-down" or "100 percent mortgage") is a great way to sell 2 A.M. infomercials, but it's rarely any use in the real world. Furthermore, as the real estate market gets hotter and hotter, there are fewer unsophisticated sellers (read: *gullible idiots*) out there who are willing to do one.

I'm speaking from experience. Yes, I've done no-money-down deals— and when you become fluent in real estate investment, some of these deals will no doubt come your way, too. They're legal and they're doable, but why would you count on doing one? The truth is, it's much easier to simply raise the capital and work within the traditional financing. If you build your business plan around these deals, it may take you six or nine months to find your first one . . . whereas you could have found an enthusiastic investor group in your first three weeks.

Simply put, there are much better ways to dip your toes into the real estate pool.

---

### Should I Become a Broker?

I meet a lot of folks who think becoming a real estate broker would be a great way to break into the field. The thing is, most of the actual brokers I know began as brokers . . . and remained brokers. Yes, you do learn about real estate through brokering, but you learn specifically from the perspective of a *salesperson*, not an investor. It's a crucial difference. The longer you spend selling real estate, the less likely you are to start buying it. For this reason, I don't advise starting work as a broker if you're serious about investing.

---

### *The Assignable Contract*

The assignable contract allows you to make money in real estate without actually owning anything—and it works. You simply find yourself a great deal . . . and then you sell it to an investor who's in a position to purchase property. If you like hustling, you enjoy being "in the field," scouting for and selling contracts can be a lot of fun.

Here's an example of how an assignable contract works. Not long ago, I ran across a great guy who was just about to put his property on the market. David was moving to England to start school, and he didn't want to be saddled with overseas assets. A **motivated seller**, David needed to sell *right now*; any delays could put a major crimp in his plans.

> **motivated seller:** Someone who's anxious to sell for any rea-
> son—financial, personal, professional, whatever.

It didn't take me long to realize I could set up a deal that would make both me *and* David very happy. I told him, "Listen. I'll take the property off your hands. No problem. We'll go into **contract**."

> **contract:** A legal document spelling out an agreement. It may or
> may not be **assignable**, depending on its specific language.
> **assignment:** A documented offer on a property that can be
> taken over by a third party if the party making the offer so
> chooses.

Then I talked to my attorney. Here's where the assignable contract differs from an ordinary real estate transaction, and it's a very important difference: I asked my attorney to insert language in the contract giving me the permission to assign the contract. Specifically, an assignable contract must spell out that the buyer is "Joe Blow *or assigned*." With this language in place, you can legally assign the contract to someone else—that is, you can pass the contract on to another party.

My attorney worked on the final arrangements, and I gave David a good-faith payment of $500 to make it clear I was serious about this property. And I signed a simple boilerplate agreement stating that in exchange for that $500, I would have the down payment in hand and be ready to close within two weeks. On that boilerplate agreement, where it was written "Seller:_____," I filled it in with "Seller: Boaz Gilad or assigned."

> **good-faith payment:** A dollar amount given by the prospective
> buyer to the seller that symbolizes a commitment to close the
> deal. Good-faith payments are common, and they can run
> anywhere from $100 to $500.

Nine times out of ten, a seller won't even notice those two little words, *or assigned*. A motivated seller, in particular, will be too excited about unloading the property to care who ultimately buys it. If your buyer does happen to ask about the clause, there are several explanations you might offer: "My partner might want to buy this property in his name," or "My limited liability company will probably purchase this property." Another option: "I'm not sure which LLC I'll purchase this property under. I need to review my finances and holdings for each LLC and see which one makes the most sense." In general, though, it's best to not even point out those two little words in to the contract.

I told David the two-week period until closing was to allow my "partner" to review the deal. In reality, I used those two weeks to set up a meeting with Erin, an investor acquaintance of mine. I told her, "Erin, I found this property. It's amazing." She heard me out, heard the price I mentioned—$80K higher than the amount I'd agreed on with David—and was thrilled. She realized how undervalued this deal really was, even at the price I'd offered her. Savvy investors, you see, won't care what goes into a scout's pocket, as long as the numbers add up. For Erin, they did.

Between us, Erin and I created what's known as a **contract vendee**. Then we showed up at the closing together at ten o'clock in the morning. Erin took ownership of the property. I did not—not even for a moment. David had a hefty check in his hands, and he was happy. Erin had a beautiful property on her hands, and she was happy. I had $80,000 in my pocket. Enough said!

> **contract vendee:** The designated purchaser of a contract. The term is also used to refer to the arrangement itself.

This kind of deal happens a lot in the real estate world. You find a sweetheart property—but you've already got so many other buildings in your portfolio, you just can't handle another one. Or maybe you need funds right away. Still, this deal looks *sooo* good . . .

## I'll Flip Ya

In the same family as an assignable contract—a property that you don't keep for yourself—is the flip.

A flipped contract is a purchase for the sake of an immediate resale to a separate party. Let's say Leslie is selling her property to me; in turn, I'm selling it to Daniel. I would purchase Leslie's property at ten o'clock in the morning and then sell the property at three that afternoon to Daniel. The easiest way to deal with a flip contract is to get the original seller—in this case, Leslie—to agree to it. Even if the seller doesn't agree, though, you can still do a deal, although it's risky. In this case, you *must* make sure that the person to whom you're flipping the property does indeed purchase it from you. If not—if your new buyer (Daniel in our story) walks away or your deal with him falls through, for whatever reason—you're stuck with the property.

And you're stuck with a hefty tax bill as well. That's the real risk of a flip: Unless you transfer ownership within 24 hours, you'll be liable for a bunch of taxes. If you do transfer the contract within that day, however, the only tax you'll pay is something called a transfer tax, which is pretty minimal (although worth including as you crunch the numbers!): On a million-dollar property, for instance, the transfer tax will run you about $3,000.

Here's one other factor to think about: You don't have to let the original owner know you're selling the contract. If, for instance, your seller is Ms. Hard-core Scrooge (most of us are), she may not be at all happy to know that you'll be selling her contract. "*What?*" she'll rant. "You're saying I could've gotten $80,000 more for this property?" A lot of deals will fall through at moments like these.

If you're dealing with a Scrooge, remember that you're under no obligation to let her know what will happen to her property after it changes hands.

---

### Selling the Sell Contract

Having trouble finding buyers for the contract you're trying to sell? Bring it to an entrepreneurs' club or real estate club. These organizations almost always feature an open-mike session at the end of their meetings. You just hop on up to the dais, hold up your contract, and state the deal succinctly: "Here's a house in the heart of the city that's worth half a million, and I have a contract for $375K. If you're interested, come talk to me in the back of the room after the meeting."

If you'd like to open up your deal to a global market, visit a real estate chat room on the World Wide Web.

# Cold Hard Cash

### *Seller Financing*

Ready for another story? Kevin was just about to retire and move to Florida. Before he could hit the Land of Sunshine and Eternal Golf Courses, though, he needed to sell the house he grew up in—he was counting on those proceeds to pay for his retirement and greens fees. His plan was to put the profits into a bank CD and live off the interest.

Not a bad plan, actually, especially because Kevin had bought his home 30-some years back for $30K—and it was now worth a million and a half.

"But Kevin," I told him, "here's the thing: If you sell this house right now, you're going to be paying a lot of capital gains taxes." Some of his gains would be exempt (as I described to you in Chapter 1), but most of them would not. With a $1.5 million price tag on his home, moreover, this was a man with a lot to lose.

"So," I continued, "let's use seller financing."

Kevin was all ears. His future was at stake.

"Here's what we'll do. Forget the bank. A bank is going to pay you *possibly* around 2 percent on a CD or a money market account, given the interest rates right now.

"Instead, *I'm* going to buy your house, and I'm going to pay you *8 percent* on your money. Every month, you're going to get this check from me, for however many years."

Well, Kevin was thrilled. Two percent of a million and a half dollars is not a bad sum. I was planning to *quadruple* that. It was risk-free for him, too: If I were to miss a payment, Kevin had the right to repossess his home.

Our two attorneys created the legal documents we needed to record a 90 percent mortgage, but rather than a bank holding it, Kevin was the mortgage holder. And for the first two years of Kevin's life in Florida, he received my monthly check: 8 percent interest only.

In the meantime, I was able to buy Kevin's beautiful suburban home with *Kevin* putting up 90 percent of the money. Once the two years were up, I'd made enough progress in my real estate career—in terms of both knowledge and profits—that I was able to refinance this property and pay Kevin back.

For two years, then, Kevin got an astronomical return on his money. And when I paid off the mortgage in full, he simply reverted to his original plan: investing in a bank CD. To this day, he chortles to his friends about what a killing he made.

I'm not sure he's ever figured out who the real winner in that deal was!

As you talk to potential sellers, then, find out why they want to sell their property. That will help you decide whether seller financing is a suitable suggestion to make. If sellers don't need the money for another purchase—or if they're buying something much smaller and much cheaper, the way empty nesters often do—seller financing can be a real win–win situation. The sellers avoid capital gains taxes as well as see a huge return on their money; you get financing (and great properties!) that you might never have been able to find or qualify for otherwise.

### *Seller Concession*

Seller concession is an agreement in which sellers agree to create a contract at a higher price than their actual asking price. It is *completely* legal, and if a property is being sold at less than market value, it can be a powerful financial tool for you, the buyer.

Let's say you find a house worth half a million dollars. You know it's this valuable because other, similar houses in the same neighborhood are currently selling for $500K apiece. This owner, however, is willing to part with her home for $400K.

Here's what you do. Ask the seller, "Can you draw up a contract that states a sale price of $450K? That way I can have $50K at closing in cash, so I can perform necessary renovations."

Take a look at the numbers. Scenario 1 involves no seller concession. Compare this with Scenario 2, in which your seller agrees to help you out:

Scenario 1

*The contract says $400K.*
*You put down $40K (10 percent) plus an estimated $20K*
*in closing costs.*
*Total investment = $60K.*


Scenario 2

*The contract says $450K.*

*You put down $45K (10 percent) plus an (over)estimated $22K in*
*closing costs.*
*Total apparent investment = $67K.*
*Then: You receive $50K in cash at the closing!*
*Total actual investment: A mere $17K.*

And remember, none of this makes any difference to the seller. At the end of the day, she receives $400K under either scenario. I try to effect seller concession in every deal I do.

## On-Property Assets

You will be amazed how much stuff people leave behind when they vacate a property. Amazed! When my wife and I bought our house, the seller—a real handyman—had left behind a basement full of beautiful tools; all they needed was some cleaning. They were worth a lot of money.

I bought another property from a trust; the owner had just passed away. For simplicity's sake, the place was being sold "as is," with all amenities intact. When I examined it, I found that the furniture was pretty worthless, but then I wandered down to the basement . . . lo and behold, a gorgeous wine cellar! As a wine connoisseur, my eyes lit up. Those wines were worth better than $15,000. And when I sold them all after purchasing the property, I kept one bottle for myself, to celebrate.

If you buy retail property, the sellers might agree to (or beg to) leave behind their merchandise, or their fixtures. Homeowners retiring to Key West will leave you their snowmobiles. Empty nesters who are downsizing their lives may be delighted to pass along room after room of antiques.

Whenever you tour a potential investment property, then, keep your eyes open for possessions that have been or might be left behind. If you spot something you can't identify or recognize the worth of, bring in an expert: A contractor. An antiques dealer. A librarian. Whatever. Find out what the goods are worth, and whether you have a realistic chance of selling them. (Be sure to ask the expert who's doing your appraisal if he or she would like to deal!) If so, the money you realize from those on-site assets can be used to reduce your investment—sometimes to almost ridiculously low amounts.

# A Myriad of Mortgages

Let's look at the rest of the picture. There are a variety of mortgages to examine, including interest-only, 5-1 ARM, 30-year fixed, and LIBOR. As time progresses, banks come up with more creative ways to finance real estate. Speak with a good mortgage broker who can find you the right product for your project, level of risk, and goals.

# Action Points: Your Credit Report

You *can* obtain financing no matter what your credit history looks like. As you'd expect, though, the spottier your credit report looks, the more hoops you'll have to jump through to get that money. (These hoops take the form of higher interest rates, among other things.) And the better your history looks, the more eager lenders will be to send funds your way.

If you don't already know exactly what's on your credit report, it's time to find out—now, *before* potential financiers have a look at it.

And the government has stepped in to help you out. In 2004, the Fair and Accurate Credit Transaction Act was passed into law. This act mandates that as of September 1, 2005, every American is entitled to a free copy of his or her credit report—from all three of the major credit reporting bureaus—absolutely free, and on an annual basis.

To obtain your own credit history, here's what you need to know:

- AnnualCreditReport.com: www.annualcreditreport.com; 877-322-8228. This is the congressionally mandated information clearinghouse.

    When you log on to AnnualCreditReport.com, you'll be able to order a copy of your credit rating from the three major credit reporting agencies: Equifax, Experian, and TransUnion. You can choose to get all three of these reports at once, or to space them out over the course of the year. All are free.

    Call or click now and have a long, close look at what you find.

Monitoring your credit reports regularly can alert you to any errors or inaccuracies that may exist. The credit bureaus oversee millions of accounts; mistakes can and do happen. You'll also have a list of every single credit account that's currently open in your name. This gives you a chance to close unused accounts and reduce your revolving credit (which can adversely affect your credit rating).

Even more critical, your credit reports can tell you if you've been the victim of identity theft—a crime that you might otherwise not detect for weeks or even months, with potentially ruinous consequences.

If you spot any problems on your report, or simply have a question about what it all means, you can contact the credit bureau in question:

- Equifax: www.equifax.com; 800-685-1111
- Experian: www.experian.com; 888-397-3742
- TransUnion: www.transunion.com; 800-916-8800

---

### Credit Report Caution

Credit reports are a hot topic these days, and with all this public attention come those folks hoping to make a buck. AnnualCreditReport.com is the *only* group you need to contact to obtain your credit history. A lot of other organizations will try to sell you subscriptions to their credit monitoring services. Now, these aren't necessarily scams—for some folks, they can be very worthwhile investments. But you are legally entitled to a free annual report. If anyone charges money for your credit report, understand that you should be getting much more than just an annual report for that fee. If you're not—or if all you're really after is that yearly report, not sophisticated monitoring services—*run, don't walk* away from the deal.

---

# 6

# The Numbers

Your calculator is about to become your best friend. It and it alone will dictate whether you have a great deal on your hands. How gorgeous the building is, its location, whether famous people partied there (or partied a little too hard)—none of that matters. The numbers and only the numbers are your guide. You buy because of the numbers.

Isn't real estate already about a hundred times easier now that you know that?

Before we get down to the figure crunching, though, there's a basic concept you need to understand. It's called cash-on-cash.

## The Easiest Way to View It All: Cash-on-Cash

Cash-on-cash is a system for analyzing potential investments—calculating your potential returns. It's a simple, conservative system that looks at money in versus money out.

Cash-on-cash compares cash out (your investment) with cash in (your net return). Here's a simplified explanation of how it works. Let's say you're looking at buying a million-dollar building that requires putting down $100K in cash. The cash-on-cash system doesn't consider the $900,000 that'll be mortgaged. It compares instead your initial investment—how much you put in, in this case $100,000—and the net profits you'll receive at the end of the year. We'll assume here that after you've paid all of this property's annual expenses—including mortgage expenses—you'll have $8,000 left over. Compare this with the $100,000 you invested initially and you'll come up with a cash-on-cash return for your potential investment of 8 percent.

**net return:** The amount of money you take in after all your expenses are paid.

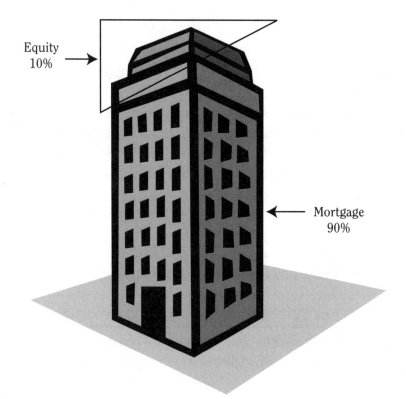

Equity
10%

Mortgage
90%

**Figure 6.1.** Ten-percent-down mortgage.

---

**Cash In:**

Income from rentals: $5,000/month

**Cash Out:**

Debt service (mortgage): $2,300/month
Expenses (see below): $2,033/month
Total cash out: $4,333/month
Net return: $667/month $\times$ 12 = $8,004/year (round to $8,000)

Now compare net return with your investment, $100K:
$8,000/$100,000 = 0.08 = 8 percent

**Note:** This is a simplified example that ignores some basic factors such as closing costs. Don't worry; you'll become more sophisticated with your cash-on-cash analyses as you continue in your investment career.

---

## What's a Good Cash-on-Cash Return?

There's no one simple figure that qualifies as a "good" return when you do your cash-on-cash analysis. (Life's never that easy, is it?) Every situation will differ, and you'll grow more and more savvy to the nuances as you gain experience. Still, I can give you some basic parameters to keep in mind. Just remember that they're guides, not rules.

Over the past 15 years, the average cash-on-cash return on a rental property in the United States has run between 6 and 8 percent. In some areas of the country, such as California, it's been as low as 2 percent.

If you're looking at a return rate of 2 percent, be afraid. Two percent is a problem. Eight percent is not. And anytime you see a return of *better* than 8 percent, drop everything to take a closer look at this property.

Now, once you've made your investment, you may find yourself going through periods when your return dips as low as 2 percent. That's when you need to remind yourself that real estate, especially rental real estate, is a long-term proposition. At the same time, if you're analyzing a potential investment property and come up with a 2 percent return on it— don't buy. Beginning investors invariably run into unexpected expenses.

You can find yourself operating in the red very quickly—almost without realizing it.

---

### Insider's Tip!

The less money you put in, the higher your return's going to be, right? If you can obtain 100 percent financing, you never put money in. Your cash-on-cash is now infinite. (But see Chapter 5 for more inside scoop on zero-down financing.)

---

## More on Income

After looking at all the cash-on-cash calculations above, a lot of you—you know who you are!—are saying right about now: *"Eight percent? That's it? Why should I work so hard for a measly 8 percent?"* In reality, the return is much higher. Let's look at why.

- You can expect *tax benefits* on your property totaling 12 to 16 percent of its value. These include depreciation, tax-deductible interest—everything you read about in Chapter 1. To be conservative, let's use the lower number here, 12 percent. Add 12 percent tax benefits to your 8 percent net return and you come up with 20 percent. Not bad, eh?

- Moreover, a cash-on-cash calculation doesn't even consider *appreciation*. The system looks at cash flow, pure and simple. But you'll remember everything I said previously about the power of leverage and appreciation. In this case, suppose you can sell the property after one year for $1.1 million. You're now looking at a return possibility of 120 percent per year. Needless to say, that's a pretty attractive figure!

- Something else: *rental income*. The cash-on-cash system doesn't take into account that over time, your rental rolls *will* go up. Sure, you may hit a dip or decrease in the market, but the overall trend will be higher.

All of these items—the tax benefits, the appreciation, the rising rental income—are bonuses, not givens. They do not figure into your cash-on-cash analysis. Why? Because *you want to be making money from the very begin-*

*ning*. So tuck these ideas into the back of your head. They're not factors you want to base your decisions on—just little extras along the road.

See the section called "Income versus Potential Income" later in this chapter for more perspective on this issue.

# More on Expenses

I'm not going to go into a lot of detail about your expenses here, for a couple of reasons. First off, the subject is large enough to fill a whole book all by itself. And second—it already has. In fact, this subject has filled all kinds of books. I call them "landlord books," and they're a terrific resource. Pick one up and you'll find every expense you've ever thought of and dozens more you'd probably *never* have thought of—three or four hundred possible expenses in all! You'll want to go through them carefully and ignore those irrelevant to your particular case—if you'll be investing in property next to the Everglades, for instance, you won't need to factor "snow shoveling" into your calculations.

My favorite landlord book is *The Landlord's Handbook* by Daniel Goodwin, Richard Rusdorf, and Barbara McNichol (Real Estate Education Company, 1998). For other possibilities, the legal section of any bookstore is a good place to begin. Or visit www.landlord.com for terrific resources, forms—you name it.

Let me give you a broad overview of the major operations and maintenance costs you're going to encounter.

### Debt Services

This is the cost of your leveraged money—in other words, your mortgage (principal *and* interest). It's always the first fee you pay. For new investors, by the way, I recommend a 30-year fixed mortgage. With one of these babies, you'll know exactly what your mortgage will cost every month, and it's set in stone—no surprises.

### Real Estate Taxes

Your broker can tell you what your real estate taxes will be. Be sure to find out if there will be an increase in real estate taxes upon purchase. Many cities calculate real estate taxes based on the *purchase* price, not the sale price. Ask the city (you can call the finance department in your area) how much you'll have to pay in taxes if your purchase price will be appreciably different from the property's asking price.

## Insurance

At a minimum, you'll want fire and **liability** insurance. Some investors also like to purchase renting insurance—if you lose rent, you're insured—but I haven't found that it's worth it. Insurance prices, of course, vary wildly, and it's worth shopping around. I recommend calling five different agents, or more, before making any decisions.

> **liability:** Something for which one is liable; an obligation, responsibility, or debt. Examples of liability would include a mortgage payment, an insurance bill, and a tax bill.

## Utilities

Utilities include gas or oil (if your property has a heating system). Please be very careful when calculating utilities: If you live in a cold area, heating costs will be the most expensive item on your list, and often your most unpredictable. In the past few years, for instance, the combination of bitter-cold winters in New York City and the rising price of oil really bit into my own profits.

## Electricity

This category includes air-conditioning systems in larger buildings, as well as electricity for the common areas—entrances, staircases or elevators, hallways, and so on.

## Sewer and Water

Call septic services in the area to know what price range you'll be dealing with. Or ask your broker, or request that the current owner show you several months' worth of bills so you can get an idea of the cost.

## Property Management

When you own property, things go wrong; that's just the nature of the beast. When you own a lot of property, a lot of things go wrong. Dealing with these problems—property management, the hands-on fixing of problems—must be factored into your cash-on-cash analysis.

You have at least three options here. They're all good, but they all make demands on your time and/or budget. Think about which one is right for you.

### Management Option #1: Yours Truly

If you'll be buying a small property and you're long on time, short on dollars, you may choose to manage it yourself. In this case, you don't need to include management fees in your cash-on-cash analysis. Understand, however, that day-to-day property maintenance can eat you, your schedule, and anything resembling a life for breakfast. Be realistic about the time demands that management can make. If you're still convinced that yours truly is your best option, see "Sweat Equity" in Chapter 5 for more thoughts and information.

### Management Option #2: The Management Company

If you're too busy for the day-to-day maintenance, or you're looking to grow quickly, you can hire a management company (aka rental company). These folks will take care of everything for you: collecting the rents, maintaining the building, responding to tenants' needs, and paying all the bills. In return, they'll charge a fee of somewhere between 6 and 10 percent of the gross (pre-expense) rental income.

If you'll be opting for professional management, be sure to include their fees in your cash-on-cash analysis. See Chapter 8 for details on selecting a management company.

### Management Option #3: The Super

I manage my own investment properties through a super. I really don't have the time or know-how to deal with the day-to-day stuff myself. Still, I want to maintain some measure of control over what happens to my tenants and my buildings. For me, then, the super is a kind of middle ground. I'm not being represented by a large, faceless, impersonal corporation—but I can still offer expert and professional attention to everyone I serve.

My super is a member of my staff. I pay him a regular, generous salary and make sure he's always equipped with a pager. Whenever something goes wrong, my super is the one who fields the complaint, and he's the one who goes out and fixes the problem. He's a sort of combination therapist-handyman—maintenance and repair with a face, a cheerful attitude, and a few decades of experience.

Good supers are worth their weight in gold. If this is the management option that's right for you, once again be sure to include your super's salary in your cash-on-cash analysis.

## A Property Buying Checklist*

The following factors should be considered when you're buying property. Rate each item on the list G—Good, F—Fair, or P—Poor. If the majority of this list isn't marked Good, have a professional inspect the property before you buy. You need to know if it's structurally sound.

### Exterior

_____ Age. This is unimportant if the property is structurally sound.

_____ Location. The most important factor in buying!

_____ Construction. Good construction is important.

_____ Drive-up appeal. This is an important factor for tenants.

_____ Size of house. Three bedrooms is best.

_____ Foundation. Check for holes, cracks, and settlement.

_____ Brickwork. Look for cracks and missing mortar.

_____ Siding. Look for loose or missing pieces.

_____ Paint. Look for peeling, chipping, blistering, and so on.

_____ Entrance porch. Examine steps, handrails, and posts.

_____ Windows and screens. Look for cracked or broken glass.

_____ Storm windows. Are they complete and caulked?

_____ Roof. A good roof is a must. Use binoculars to inspect it.

_____ Gutters and downspouts. Check for holes and leaks.

_____ Chimney. Look for tilting, loose, or missing bricks.

_____ Walls and fences. Are they structurally sound?

_____ Garage. Check doors, roof, siding, and windows.

_____ Driveway and sidewalks. Look for holes and cracks.

\_\_\_\_ Grounds and landscaping. Locate the property lines.

\_\_\_\_ Proper drainage. Will rain flow away from the house?

**Interior**

\_\_\_\_ Structure. Does the property feel solid?

\_\_\_\_ Floor plan. Unusual floor plans are less desirable.

\_\_\_\_ Floors. Check for level. Notice movement and squeaking as you walk.

\_\_\_\_ Stairs. Look for loose treads and loose handrails.

\_\_\_\_ Plumbing. Look for leaks. Flush the toilets. Turn on the faucets.

\_\_\_\_ Heating system. Type, age, last time serviced.

\_\_\_\_ Water heater. Look for leaks and rusting. Age?

\_\_\_\_ Electrical system. Is it adequate for the property?

\_\_\_\_ Air-conditioning. Type, age, last time serviced?

\_\_\_\_ General layout. Is the floor plan typical for the area?

\_\_\_\_ Kitchen. Adequate shelves and counter space?

\_\_\_\_ Bathrooms. Check for cracks in tile and signs of leaks.

\_\_\_\_ Living room. Is it large enough?

\_\_\_\_ Dining room. Is it large enough?

\_\_\_\_ Bedrooms. Check size and closet space.

\_\_\_\_ Storage. Is the storage space adequate?

\_\_\_\_ Windows. Check to see if they open and close easily.

\_\_\_\_ Doors. Do they open and close properly? Are the locks good?

* Adapted from "Exterior and Interior Inspection," © 1997 by WWV, Inc. All Rights Reserved.

## Rainy-Day Funds

Property expenses don't end with day-to-day problem solving; they continue into long-term, major building maintenance expenditures. These are a bit of a dirty little secret in the real estate world; you'll hardly ever hear brokers mention them when they're going through the numbers with you. But it's critical that you include these expenses in your calculations. They can make you or break you.

You must keep money aside for every unit in every building you own. As time progresses, things will break: windows, appliances, plumbing, what have you.

And you need to keep a separate rainy-day fund for the building itself—each building you own. You'll need a new roof every 10 years; a portion of the boiler must be replaced every seven years. Trees and shrubs will die. Concrete will crumble, paint peel, foundations sag. The wall-to-wall shag carpeting that made your lobby so *hot*, so *now* 10 years ago will suddenly make your lobby look . . . so *10-years-ago*. And so on, ad infinitum. If you don't put small amounts of money aside *now* for use later, your building will deteriorate—and with it your reputation.

## *Vacancies*

When your bank or lending institution calculates the value of your building, it will automatically include a vacancy rate of 5 percent (or more). You need to do this, too. You never know when a tenant might leave, and if one does, you never know how long it might take you to rent the unit again. If it's the middle of winter, you could be waiting a long time—nobody likes to face the thought of moving when it's below zero and streets are icy. Moreover, even if you've got a new tenant waiting in the wings, it could take you a week or more to repaint, repair, and clean the apartment in question.

Or here's another thing that could happen: You could get stuck with a problem tenant who won't (or can't) pay the rent. You do have some legal recourse in this kind of situation, but they take time. And until the problem is resolved, you may be going without income.

Assume a vacancy rate right in your initial expense calculations, and all this lost income is accounted for.

---

### Insider's Tip!

If you have a foreclosure on your credit report, it will be very difficult for you to get a mortgage. A bankruptcy, on the other hand, is less problematic—especially given that more than 2.3 percent of Americans declare bankruptcy every year. You can clean up your credit from a bankruptcy more effectively than you can from a foreclosure. Do whatever you can to avoid foreclosure!

---

# Action Points: Putting Together
# Your Cash-on-Cash Analysis

By now you've zeroed in on one, two, or more potential investments that fit your niche and your neighborhood. (And if you haven't, for Pete's sake stop reading and go find some!) Well, it's now time to stop asking yourself if these properties are right for you and start seeing what the numbers say. *Do not pursue a property unless the numbers add up.*

The spreadsheets that follow—I've included four of them, for you to analyze four separate potential investments—will take you through a cash-on-cash analysis. Plug in the real numbers from the properties you're looking at.

The best way to get these numbers is to ask the seller (or the seller's agent) to provide copies of the previous two years' bills. You can also check with the broker you're dealing with, examine newspapers and Web sites, and look at similar buildings in the same neighborhood and size range.

# The Red Zone

So you took the leap, bought a property . . . and things are not going the way you'd hoped. Maybe it's bad tenants, or a change in the market, or unforeseen expenses—say, a rotting foundation beam that no one was aware of. Your own management decisions could even be to blame. Whatever the case, a situation that you thought you had firmly in hand has suddenly passed out of your control, and there you are: losing money. If you're operating in the red—whether the cause be internal or external, something you had control over or not—drop everything and deal with it *now*.

Your first step is to determine if the problem is a temporary one—something you can take care of in the next few months. A deadbeat tenant, say, or a maintenance issue that's solvable. If there's light at the end of the tunnel, your best move is to just remind yourself of your long-term commitment and hang in there as best you can.

*If*, however, there's a problem on your property that won't realistically be gone in two to three months—*get rid of the property.* Even if you're not

| Property Report | Units | Start Date | End Date |
|---|---|---|---|
| Address: | | | |
| | Store | | |
| Total Rent | | | |
| $ | – Monthly | | |
| | | | |
| Fixed Expenses: | | | |
| R.E. Taxes | | Paid by Bank | |
| Company Management | 2% | $ | – |
| Water/Sewer | | | |
| Maintenance | | $ | – |
| Super | | $ | – |
| Insurance | | | |
| Mortgage | | | |
| Variable Expenses: | | | |
| Repairs | | $ | – |
| Elevator | | N/A | |
| Electric | | | |
| Gas | | N/A | |
| Fuel | | | |
| Management | 8% | $ | – |
| Renovation | | | |
| Legal | | $ | – |
| Eviction | | | |
| Bank Fees | | | |
| Constructions | | N/A | |
| Vacancy | 10% | $ | – |
| Refi | | N/A | |
| Total: | | $ | – |
| Cash flow | | | – |
| | MONTHLY | | – |

**Figure 6.2.** Cash flow report.

# The Numbers

| Property Report | Units | Start Date | End Date |
|---|---|---|---|
| Address: | | | |
| | Store | | |
| Total Rent | | | |
| $ | – Monthly | | |
| | | | |
| Fixed Expenses: | | | |
| R.E. Taxes | | Paid by Bank | |
| Company Management | 2% | $ | – |
| Water/Sewer | | | |
| Maintenance | | $ | – |
| Super | | $ | – |
| Insurance | | | |
| Mortgage | | | |
| Variable Expenses: | | | |
| Repairs | | $ | – |
| Elevator | | N/A | |
| Electric | | | |
| Gas | | N/A | |
| Fuel | | | |
| Management | 8% | $ | – |
| Renovation | | | |
| Legal | | $ | – |
| Eviction | | | |
| Bank Fees | | | |
| Constructions | | N/A | |
| Vacancy | 10% | $ | – |
| Refi | | N/A | |
| Total: | | $ | – |
| Cash flow | | | – |
| | MONTHLY | | – |

**Figure 6.2.** Cash flow report (continued).

| Property Report | Units | Start Date | End Date |
|---|---|---|---|
| Address: | | | |
| | Store | | |
| Total Rent | | | |
| $ | – Monthly | | |
| | | | |
| Fixed Expenses: | | | |
| R.E. Taxes | | Paid by Bank | |
| Company Management | 2% | $ | – |
| Water/Sewer | | | |
| Maintenance | | $ | – |
| Super | | $ | – |
| Insurance | | | |
| Mortgage | | | |
| Variable Expenses: | | | |
| Repairs | | $ | – |
| Elevator | | N/A | |
| Electric | | | |
| Gas | | N/A | |
| Fuel | | | |
| Management | 8% | $ | – |
| Renovation | | | |
| Legal | | $ | – |
| Eviction | | | |
| Bank Fees | | | |
| Constructions | | N/A | |
| Vacancy | 10% | $ | – |
| Refi | | N/A | |
| Total: | | $ | – |
| Cash flow | | | – |
| | MONTHLY | | – |

**Figure 6.2.** Cash flow report (continued).

# The Numbers

| Property Report | Units | | Start Date | End Date |
|---|---|---|---|---|
| Address: | | | | |
| | | Store | | |
| Total Rent | | | | |
| $ | – | Monthly | | |
| | | | | |
| Fixed Expenses: | | | | |
| R.E. Taxes | | | Paid by Bank | |
| Company Management | 2% | $ | | – |
| Water/Sewer | | | | |
| Maintenance | | $ | | – |
| Super | | $ | | – |
| Insurance | | | | |
| Mortgage | | | | |
| Variable Expenses: | | | | |
| Repairs | | $ | | – |
| Elevator | | N/A | | |
| Electric | | | | |
| Gas | | N/A | | |
| Fuel | | | | |
| Management | 8% | $ | | – |
| Renovation | | | | |
| Legal | | $ | | – |
| Eviction | | | | |
| Bank Fees | | | | |
| Constructions | | N/A | | |
| Vacancy | 10% | $ | | – |
| Refi | | N/A | | |
| Total: | | $ | | – |
| Cash flow | | | | – |
| | | MONTHLY | | – |

**Figure 6.2.** Cash flow report (continued).

making money on the sale, and no matter the time or effort you've invested in this building. When a property is a loser, it's a loser. The longer you wait, the more money you'll lose. It's better to work for "nothing" for six months, sell the property at the same price you paid for it, and return the money to all your financial backers than it is to dodge investor phone calls for six months while your property drains the life out of you and your bank account.

One of the greatest dangers that first-time investors face is getting too attached to their first property. They try desperately to fix a situation that's unfixable because they can't face the thought of letting go. Ultimately, however, they have no choice. Companies like mine are only too ready to swoop in and buy these properties at deep discounts because the newbies simply waited too long.

Don't do this. Learn to let go. You never want to get overly attached to your first property—or to any property. Remember, the land is not "yours." Focus on the numbers and you won't get burned.

Another crucial point to keep in mind: You can't simply dump a bad property in the market the way you could, say, a stock. No matter what the market looks like, selling a property takes time—and if you're facing foreclosure, you may not have that time. The longer you wait, the more you lose.

Bottom line: Don't operate in the red. Sell it, walk away from it, move on to something new.

But don't wallow in your mistakes, either. This particular investment may have been a failure, but you're not. Let it go and find your next investment.

## Income versus Potential Income

Do not buy a property based on its potential income. Period.

There is one single exception to this rule, and you can no doubt figure it out for yourself: It is acceptable to base a buy-decision on potential income when you'll be leading a major construction, renovation, or **turnaround** on the property. In these cases, obviously, the current income is minimal—if not zero. So you'll have to make some predictions about potential income to complete your analysis. For more on this exception, see the "Construction Investments" section below.

# The Numbers

> **turnaround:** Restoring a poorly managed property to quality management; bringing a property that is not up to market rent, up to market rent.

I gave a series of seminars recently in San Diego, and there I met James, an area dentist. He raced up to me after my presentation to tell me how excited he was about his very first investment property—a condo. He added proudly that he needed to put in "only" $700 per month to cover his expenses on the building. "Because in three years," he continued blithely, "I know the condo will be worth a lot of money."

"How do you know that?" I asked.

James replied, "Well, look what happened to it in the *last* three years. Look how much it went up in value."

I could only cringe. While it's true that San Diego is among the fastest-growing real estate markets in the country, sometimes hot real estate markets are like soufflés: They rise very quickly, but they also fall very quickly. And there's nothing but hot air inside.

*Do not count on appreciation*. Appreciation is speculative in nature. Cash flow is king. Mix up these two priorities and you're setting yourself up for a nightmare.

James didn't care about his cash flow—only about his speculation. I tried to talk some sense into him, but I'm afraid he was too revved up for my advice to sink in. I never found out what happened to him.

I can guess, though. A simpler term for *potential investment* is *bad investment*.

Another story: In 2002, the New York City rental market was very hot, and my seminars were crammed with investors and investor hopefuls. Among them were Doug and Evelyn, a bright young couple who'd just taken the plunge by purchasing a 10-family apartment building.

I liked this energetic pair, so I was deeply dismayed when they showed me the analysis they'd made leading up to their buy-decision. It was all based on a *projected* yearly increase in rent. "See, look at this column," Doug said, pointing to the set of figures representing rents from the *previous* three years, 1999 through 2002. They had indeed climbed dramatically. And all the subsequent numbers were based on the idea that this climb would continue every year thereafter.

Once again, I tried to inject a note of caution into the conversation. Once again, these newbie investors were just too dazzled by their potential profits to hear me.

I kept tabs on Doug and Evelyn over the next few years. And in 2003, the rental market went through an abrupt about-face. Suddenly rents stopped vaulting upward; they were stagnating or even going down. Investors citywide were unable to find tenants willing to pay the prices they were charging.

But Doug and Evelyn were in love with the rents they'd projected. More than in love, they *needed* those rents to attain the profits they were expecting. So when some of their tenants moved out—the way tenants will—the young couple put the units on the market at the inflated rents they were counting on.

Doug and Evelyn's high-priced apartments remained vacant for many, many months. And every day those apartments sat empty, the couple lost even more money. When they finally woke up and recognized what had happened, they started reducing their rents. By that time, unfortunately, the overall city rental market was glutted with vacancies.

Last I heard, Doug and Evelyn had taken their rents all the way down to 2002 levels. They'd found a single new tenant at these prices, but four of their apartments remained vacant.

Bottom line #1: *Rent those apartments*. Even if you have to throw in a free parking space. Rent them.

Bottom line #2: Another name for *potential investment* is *bad investment*.

---

### Insider's Tip!

If you're investing in a rent-stabilized city, you may be reluctant to reduce your "official" rents lest the regulations prevent you from ever raising them as quickly as you might like. Here's a way around the dilemma: Don't lower the price listed on your leases. Instead, offer potential tenants one month's free rent.

---

# Construction Investments

What if the investment you're considering isn't an existing profit maker, but a future one—a property you're hoping to build, or perform major renovations on? I meet a lot of real estate hopefuls who are weighing such purchases. For good reason: Construction investments can be among the most lucrative out there.

So let's look at them. And here's the main thing you need to know: If you're thinking about construction, the cash-on-cash analysis model stays intact, but with some additional considerations.

Ready to crunch some numbers?

Construction is calculated per square foot. So your first step is to calculate the cost of the land you're looking at per square foot. Let's say you're contemplating the purchase of a lot that measures 25 by 100 feet. Zoning for the area permits you to build "times three"—that is, you can construct a building up to three times the size of the lot:

$$25 \times 100 = 2,500$$

$$2,500 \times 3 = 7,500$$

You can put in a building of up to 7,500 square feet.

> **zoning:** The regulations governing what kinds of buildings, sizes of buildings, and density of buildings (square footage compared with lot size) are allowed in a particular neighborhood. Zoning is determined and enforced at the town or city level.

More assumptions: Let's say you're buying this lot for $450,000. Your next step is to divide this price by the potential square feet:

$$\$450,000 / 7,500 = \$60$$

You're buying this land for $60 per square foot.

Now it's time to calculate the cost of construction. And this is where predictions grow more variable and less reliable, because there is no set number for construction costs. You can put up structures that range anywhere from the lowest quality—frame homes with low-end finishing—all the way up to marble-and-mahogany villas that may cost mega-thousand bucks per square foot. You must determine the quality and style of construction that your project requires *before* attacking a spreadsheet.

> ### Insider's Tip!
>
> I recommend building above the average standard in the neighborhood. People always appreciate quality, and it helps you build a name for yourself. Also, if there happens to an oversupply of housing in the market, your property will be among the first ones sold or rented.

The cost of construction is split into two categories. *Hard costs* include all the tangible items in the structure—the items you can actually touch and/or see on the site—wood, glass, metal, labor, and so on. Here is a breakdown of some of the hard costs you'll be dealing with:

- Real estate taxes
- Company management
- Water/sewer
- Maintenance
- Superintendent ("Super")
- Insurance
- Mortgage

The second element, unsurprisingly, is called *soft costs*. Soft costs are all those intangibles involved in your project: **application fees**, financing fees, architectural and planning costs, **carrying costs**, and so forth:

- Repairs
- Elevator
- Electric
- Gas and fuel
- Renovation
- Legal fees
- Bank fees
- Vacancy (anticipate 10 percent, conservatively)

**application fees:** Fees that must be paid for banking services (such as mortgages) and for local licenses to perform construction.

**carrying costs:** Total expenses that must be paid during the period of "no income," which carry you through until income is generated. Prime among carrying cost are the real estate taxes you'll be paying on the lot during the construction process.

A good general rule to know is this: *Soft costs are usually equal to one-third of the hard costs*. If you're expecting your project's hard costs to come out at $1.35 million, for example, it's appropriate to project soft costs of $450,000.

Divide hard costs by square footage to obtain your total hard costs per square foot. Do the same with soft costs. In our example:

Hard costs = $1,350,000 / 7,500 = $180 per square foot

Soft costs = $450,000 / 7,500 = $60 per square foot

The next step is to add it all up: hard costs, soft costs, land costs. This will give you the total cost of construction.

Hard + Soft + Land = Total construction costs

In our example, this means:

$180 + $60 + $60 = $300 per square foot

You're now *almost* ready to calculate your potential profit. There are two crucial points to consider first, however:

1. Not all the square footage in the building is saleable. Typically, only *80 to 85 percent of a property's square footage is saleable.* If you've got 7,500 square feet, then, only 6,000 to 6,375 of those feet are going to be profit makers for you. The rest will be used in common areas: walls and stairways, elevators, parking, lobby, offices, and the like. (In larger buildings, this figure can be a bit higher than 85 percent.)

2. More construction properties are sold than rented—typically, the process is *buy, build, sell*. So don't forget to calculate the *closing costs and broker fees* you'll be paying when it comes time to make your sale.

---

### Insider's Tip!

When you sell your construction properties, be sure that the fee your broker charges you is calculated on the saleable square footage, not the total building square footage. In other words, calculate the broker's commission from *your* net—after your expenses.

---

Now you're ready to determine potential profit. Take a look at how much money square footage is generally being sold for in the area in question—the going rate. The difference between the two is your profit:

$$\text{Sales} - \text{Cost} = \text{Profit}$$

So . . . here's the final cash-on-cash look at our sample construction investment:

You buy a property of 25' × 100'—2,500 square feet.
It's zoned for three times the lot size, or 7,500 square feet, at $60 per square foot.
Add hard costs of $180 per square foot.
Add soft costs of $60 per square foot.
Total cost of land plus hard and soft costs is $300 per square foot.

You take a look at your neighborhood and determine that property typically sells for around $600 per square foot. Your first thought here might be this: *Hey, I'm going to be making $300 per square foot!*

Alas, that's not the case at all. Here's why:

Start by determining your total cost. For this property, 7,500 square feet times $300 per square foot equals a total cost $2.25 million.

*But* out of the 7,500 square feet, only (let's say) 85 percent is saleable—6,375 square feet of profit-generating property.

*And* you'll pay a 5 percent commission to your broker. This cuts your profit-making property down to 95 percent (0.95) of that saleable total:

# The Numbers

$$6{,}375 \text{ square feet} \times 0.95 = 6{,}056.25 \text{ square feet}$$

Your net profit is thus based on those 6,056.25 profit-making square feet.

*Now* you can calculate your potential sales. Multiply your profitable square feet by $600 (the going rate for the area):

$$6{,}056.25 \times \$600 = \$3{,}633{,}750$$

Subtract your total costs of $2.25 million (as determined above):

$$\$3{,}633{,}750 - \$2{,}250{,}000 = \$1{,}383{,}750$$

There's your potential profit: $1,383,750.

But you're not quite ready to put the calculator away yet. (Sorry!) Let's say you borrowed 80 percent of the money—80 percent financing, or 80 percent LTV (loan to value). Your loan total is thus

$$\$2{,}250{,}000 \times 0.80 = \$1{,}800{,}000$$

And your cash investment—20 percent, the amount of money you put down—is

$$\$2{,}250{,}000 - \$1{,}800{,}000 = \$450{,}000$$

Compare your potential profit with your cash investment:

$$\$1{,}383{,}750 \,/\, \$450{,}000 = 3.075$$

Look at that number again. You're looking at a *307.5 percent return* over, say, two years.

This is why people do construction.

However (you didn't think you'd get away without a *however* here, did you?), construction also involves any number of variables—and believe me when I tell you that these can vary wildly. Every single one of the numbers you plugged into the equations above can double, triple, or be cut in half overnight. The returns on construction are often huge, then, but so are the risks. I strongly recommend that you get some real estate experience under your belt before investigating construction as a viable income source.

But do be sure to consider it a bit farther down your road!

# 7

# Closing
# the Deal

I worked on one particular deal for what seemed like forever. Everyone I knew was convinced this deal was never going to go through—my attorney, the real estate broker, the seller, my barber, the kid across the hall—everyone. "This deal is *dead*," they told me. "Walk away. Find something else." The broker called me to complain that he'd put a down payment on a new Jeep, but now he was sure he'd never get his hands on that vehicle: My deal was never going to happen.

"Oh, for Pete's sake," I replied, "I'm going to *make* this happen. If you want to talk about how you can help, great. But if all you're going to do is complain, I'm going to hang up on you right now. I don't need that attitude."

It took me 10 months, but I closed the deal. I bought the property for $752,000, refinanced it for $1.3 million after 14 months, and sold it for $1.7 million after 21 months.

The moral of the story is this: Keep on working. Now, it's true that you can't expect to close every deal. Some will fall through, some won't work, some should never have seen the light of day to begin with. If a deal is truly dead, walk away from it.

Just don't walk away too soon.

I was born and raised in Israel, and like most Israelis, I served a required stint in the military. The Israeli army has a critical rule that it drums into its soldiers over and over again: If someone is hurt, you help him, and *you do not stop* until a doctor pronounces him dead. No matter how hopeless the situation looks, no matter how strongly you're convinced *This man is gone*, you don't stop trying to bring him back to life until the doctor says, "He's gone."

I realize that this is a pretty stark image, but it's one I take to heart. When it comes to real estate, it's the attitude you need to have: *It's not over till it's over. It's never dead till it's dead.*

# The Big Picture

Closing a deal is a very fragile process. Things can go awry at any step along the way. You must have a complete understanding of both the players and the process to make sure you're on top of everything throughout.

## The Players

Because closing a deal involves so many people, there are lots of egos to be appeased. Understanding the roles of the key players is vital:

- Buyer
- Seller
- Real estate agent(s)
- Buyer's attorney
- Seller's attorney
- Mortgage broker
- Financier
- Appraiser
- Engineer
- Title company

## The Process

Put all these people (and their egos) into a deal and here's what *should* happen:

1. Offer
2. Acceptance
3. Attorney-talk (also known as the sandbox)
4. Contract signing
5. Mortgage commitment
6. Title search
7. Appraiser inspection
8. Engineer inspection
9. Walk-through
10. Closing

Let's make sure this is what *does* happen.

# Let's Make a Deal: A Who's Who

On one side of the room is you, the buyer—you and any investors you're working with. If you've been dealing with real estate agents, they're along for the ride, too.

On the other side are the sellers plus their agents (if any). And the more you know about your sellers, the better. Why are they selling? Might they change their minds? Why? What can you do to make them more comfortable? The more at ease the sellers are with you, your team, your deal, the whole process, the less likely they are to raise objections or obstacles. Take care of your sellers.

However . . . you need to know that if and when you and the sellers have retained attorneys, your attorney won't be legally allowed to talk to the sellers directly, and vice versa. No, you're not going to be arrested for breaching this rule, but it could be grounds to invalidate any contract. While the process is ongoing, you can deal only with the sellers' attorneys. You can't even speak to the sellers on the phone at this time unless both attorneys are in on the call as well—and many sellers will not want to talk without their attorneys present.

Talk to your attorney about everything these rules entail. But my basic advice remains the same no matter how you communicate with your sellers: Think about them. Put them at ease. Make them happy. Take care of them. Be good to your sellers.

*When I was starting out, my attorney and I were at a closing with a perfectly amiable seller. There were still a few small items to negotiate regarding the title. The seller had brought his wife and four young children to the closing, and the kids were making a terrific ruckus. Despite the seller's pleasant demeanor, we could see him getting irritated—his babies were screaming in the background. Not a good situation.*

*So we requested that the heat be turned up in the boardroom we were in. Within 10 minutes, all four children were asleep . . . and we had a lovely closing.*

## The Attorney

Different states have different laws and regulations when it comes to using attorneys to close real estate deals. Some require their presence (New York is one); others don't (California). You'll need to research the laws in the state you'll be doing your work in.

That said, I believe attorneys are crucial for the deal. They're there to protect you. Think about it—that's their whole job, to take care of you and protect your interests. Who wouldn't want that? My advice is to use an attorney no matter the regulations you're dealing with.

At the same time, don't ever stop looking after your own interests, too. Here's what I mean: Attorneys are trained, from law school onward, into a particular way of thinking that's often known as the "sandbox mentality." (It was my own lawyer who told me this secret. I believe him.) Ever seen two kids playing in a sandbox? "That's *my* toy." "No, it's *my* toy!" "No, *mine!*" And they keep pulling the toy back and forth until, eventually, it breaks.

Do not let your attorney run the show or negotiate for you. You're running the show. Yes, it's crucial to listen to your lawyer's advice and consider it carefully. But *this is your deal.* Most attorneys are not entrepreneurs, and they're not businesspeople. They'll pull a deal back and forth until it breaks. At one of my closings, my former attorney just walked away, trying to make a point; I had to run after her and beg her to come back to the table. It's simply the way lawyers operate—the way they're trained to operate.

You're the one whose money and energy and reputation are on the line here. You're the one who's going to take the risks and reap the profits. I can no longer count how many times my attorney has told me, "What you're doing right now is very risky." Bless the man; that's what I pay him for. And I take his objections seriously.

But in the end I almost always give him the same reply: "Thank you for protecting me, thank you *so much*, and I'm going to make this decision anyway. I know what I'm doing; I'm willing to take the risk." Don't forget that at the sale point, your lawyer will walk away with a flat fee . . . and you will walk away with a *deal*.

## The Mortgage Broker and Mortgage Holder

Someone at the closing is going to have to come up with the money. As the buyer, you'll pony up a percentage; the financier will hand over the rest. Your mortgage broker is the one who put the two of you together to make your beautiful deals. See Chapter 8, "Your Team," for a complete rundown on all these players.

Once again: Take care of them. Respect them. Be good to them. Do everything possible to ensure a great relationship with the people who give you money. You want them to feel comfortable doing business with you— so comfortable that they'll do lots more of it.

## The Appraisers

The appraisers are those folks who analyze your potential property and decide if it's worth what you think it is. Some are real estate specialists who can look over the price tag; some are engineers who'll examine the physical plant itself, looking for problems.

You hardly ever have to worry about hiring appraisers yourself: The bank will do it anyway. In fact, even if you do hire your own appraisers—of whatever flavor—the bank is liable to simply ignore their opinion and send in its own people.

Trust them. Banks are very conservative—as well they should be, since they're putting up 80, 90, or 100 percent of the money for the deal. They want to make sure they're lending against the right property. If there's a problem with the deal, or with the building, the bank's appraisers are either going to find it or face losing their reputations, if not their licenses.

In fact, the only problem you might have with a bank's appraisers is that they're *too* conservative. If you're trying to buy a property for $500K, the bank's appraisers might come back and tell you, "But it's only worth $400K." This is a case where it might be worthwhile to have an appraiser of your own—someone who can go out and find **comps** supporting that higher price, if you know it's worth it.

> **comp:** Short for *comparable*, a comp is a real estate transaction that took place in the same neighborhood, in the same time frame, and for the same type of property as yours. Comparing your deal with similar deals allows an appraiser to determine if the price is appropriate.

## The Title Company

The title company has several jobs. First, it makes sure that a property's seller does in fact legally own the property. And yes, that sounds so basic it's almost silly—remember all those "Hey buddy, want to buy the Brooklyn Bridge" jokes?—but be assured that it's not. I've seen it happen. Sometimes it's a con pure and simple; other times it involves legal technicalities that invalidate ownership. The title company is there to spare you these heartaches.

The title company also provides title insurance—a sort of warranty of its own work. If there's a **lien** on your property—say, a previous owner owes $20K in back taxes—and the title company's research failed to reveal it before the sale went through, title insurance mandates that the *title company* pays this lien, not you.

> **lien:** A claim against a property. A lien gives a creditor the right to take a property if you don't pay a debt. Liens can be consensual (including mortgages and home equity loans) and nonconsensual (including liens for unpaid taxes and contractors).

These same folks are also going to find out if there are **violations** on the property—and there often are. Violations can be as inconsequential as a broken window or a run-in with a local vandal; they can also involve huge issues like faulty boilers or hazardous waste.

> **violation:** Any instance in which a property fails to meet local, state, or national regulations or laws.

Sounds bad, right? Not necessarily. Violations can be a great thing. Because violations can be fixed.

A quick word of advice before we continue: Do not try to understand the violations yourself. It'll never happen. Hire an **expediter** to go the authorities—the regulators in charge of building codes—and find out what needs to be done to get these suckers fixed.

> **expediter:** A real estate professional who specializes in expediting the investment process in the municipality—by obtaining permits, paying fees, removing violations, registering rents, and so on. Your expediter will be your liaison to the local and state municipalities.

*Not long ago I found a magnificent property—great building, great deal, everything about this place made me happy. When I got the purchase ball rolling, however, the title company found that the property had 246 violations on its record. Two hundred and forty-six! That title report looked like an encyclopedia.*

*First thing I said was, "Whoa, that's scary." Then I sat down to look at it, along with Ruben, my expediter. Lesson number one from this story came when we glanced down the list and saw that 18 of the violations involved the building's elevator.*

*The building has no elevator.*

*Someone in the Buildings Department had misfiled a report. Okay: We now had 228 violations as well as a new appreciation of how important it is to double-check everything related to a transaction.*

*Lesson number two happened after Ruben finished all his research into the remaining violations. A little nervously, I asked him what it would cost to get everything fixed and a clear title.*

*"About thirty grand," he told me.*

*I said, "Hmmmm."*

*Then I got in touch with the building's owner and set up a date at the negotiating table. There my lawyer and I went through the title report with him, page by page, violation by violation. "Wow," I said. "Oh, dear," I said. "Oh, no," I said.*

*After we finished, there was a silence. "Listen," I said, "I can't do this. This is too much. I like your property, but I can't buy it without a clear title."*

*I could see the horror in this owner's face. Chances were he'd already packed up his goods and called the movers and closed the deal on a new place for himself. "What can I do?" he said. "Is there anything I can do?"*

*"Take $100K off the price," I told him.*

*He agreed to take $70K off.*

*That's the great thing about violations.*

---

### Insider's Tip!

If a property's record indicates environmental violations, *run don't walk* away from the deal. Unless you *really* know what you're doing, these issues—anything from a leaky oil tank to the illegal dumping of toxic chemicals—can be a nightmare you never wake up from.

---

## Let's Make a Deal: The Process

So those are the players. Let's turn to the play.

And this is where things get tricky. Back in the beginning of this chapter, I gave you a nice, organized, step-by-step list of the closing process. Right? Forget it. Real estate is about people, and people will always defy categorization. The only rule people ever follow is the one that says *People never follow rules.*

The first thing to understand about the closing process is that you'll never understand the closing process. It'll always surprise you.

# Closing the Deal

What follows, then, is a quick rundown of what to expect. You've just got to promise me never to expect it.

## Act I: The Offer–The Binder– The Acceptance–The Sandbox

So you've found your deal. Congratulations! Sit back and enjoy. For a nanosecond. Then roll up your sleeves, because the hard part hasn't even started yet.

Step one is to make an offer on the property. You can do this through a real estate broker or directly with the owner. I always prefer to talk to the owner if possible—if the broker is present, too, that's fine—because I find that person-to-person communication is more effective. Speaking through a broker can be like that old game of Telephone: By the time your message gets to the seller, it's garbled. Besides, you will always be your own best representative.

---

### Insider's Tip!

When you make your offer, the first number you put out there should be so low, even you feel uncomfortable with it. Once that first number is on the table, you have nowhere to negotiate but up.

---

Always strengthen your offer by presenting it with a **binder check**, generally 1 percent of the deal. If your offer is half a million, then, you'd give a binder check of $5,000. The moment they deposit the check, there's at least an informal agreement that you're going to be allowed to purchase the property. Now, this is not proof that would necessarily stand up in court, but it's still a strong indication of both parties' intentions—one that'd be difficult to fight. A binder check is a way of saying, *I'm really interested in your property. I'm not some guy off the street—I'm serious. I'm serious enough to hand you money.*

> **binder check:** A check that binds a deal, generally 1 percent of the purchase price.

By the way, there's nothing set in stone about that "1 percent" figure. You can make your binder check as large or small as you deem appropriate.

I recommend going as small as possible—you never know what's going to happen.

> *I once attended a Dolf de Roos real estate seminar at which he recommended that we each walk around with $1,000 cash in our pockets for a few weeks to "enhance our relationship with money." I usually carry about $20, if that, so this was definitely a new experience for me!*
>
> *A few days later, my broker and I happened to be in Jersey looking at a property. This place fit right into what I was looking for, so on the spot I asked my broker, "Can you introduce me to the owner? I'm ready to talk." Once the hellos were said, I shook Vin's hand and placed a verbal offer.*
>
> *Vin was a bit taken aback by my number. "That's quite a bit lower than I expected," he said. "I really thought I'd make more from this place. There are other offers—some folks came around and expressed interest."*
>
> *"Yes, but I'm serious," I countered. I reached into my pocket for my roll of money, then peeled off $500 cash and laid it on the table. "Here's five hundred dollars," I told Vin. "I'd like to go into contract—and if I don't get a contract to you in the next three days, you can keep the cash."*
>
> *Vin was so impressed by my commitment to making this deal happen (and a bit shell-shocked by the $500 on the table) that he agreed to my low offer. Vin's property ended up being a good deal for me: We purchased it without any glitches, did some light renovation, and sold it for a $90,000 profit in four months.*
>
> *Well, I'd definitely enhanced my relationship with money! (But just so you know: I've gone back to my old system of $20 in the pocket. Hey, this is the real world.)*

So: You've put in your bid and added a check. And the sellers have accepted both. Now what?

# Closing the Deal

Time for you to exit stage left and bring in the attorneys. Your lawyers and the sellers' lawyers will now jump into the sandbox (see "The Attorney," above) and hammer out all the specific details of a submit offer. (See Figure 7.1 for a sample form you might use.) This isn't the actual purchase (yet);

**SUBMIT OFFER**

| Date: | | Listing Agent: | | | Selling Agent: | | |
|---|---|---|---|---|---|---|---|
| Property: | | | | Apt.: | | Asking Price: | $ |
| **Buyer 1:** | | | | **Buyer 2:** | | | |
| Address: | | | | Address: | | | |
| Rent ☐ | Own ☐ | How Long? | | Rent ☐ | Own ☐ | How Long? | |
| Employer: | | | | Employer: | | | |
| Position: | | | | Position: | | | |
| Hire Date: | | | | Hire Date: | | | |
| Annual Salary: | $ | | | Annual Salary: | $ | | |
| Annual Bonus: | $ | | | Annual Bonus: | $ | | |
| Other Income: | $ | | | Other Income: | $ | | |
| **Total Income:** | $ | | | **Total Income:** | $ | | |

| Assets | Buyer 1 | Buyer 2 | Liabilities | Buyer 1 | Buyer 2 |
|---|---|---|---|---|---|
| Cash in Banks | $ | $ | Mortgages on Real Estate | $ | $ |
| Other Liquid Assets | $ | $ | Installment Loans (e.g., auto) | $ | $ |
| Stocks/Bonds | $ | $ | Other Accounts Payable | $ | $ |
| Retirement Accts. | $ | $ | Credit Card Balances | $ | $ |
| Real Estate Owned | $ | $ | Unpaid Taxes | $ | $ |
| Other Assets | $ | $ | Other Debts | $ | $ |
| Total Assets | $ | $ | Total Liabilities | $ | $ |
| **Combined Assets** | $ | | **Combined Liabilities** | $ | |

| Purchase Price Offered: | | All Cash ☐ | or Financing: | 75% ☐ | 80% ☐ | 90% ☐ | Other: |
|---|---|---|---|---|---|---|---|
| Total Cash Down: | | | Closing Date: | | | | |
| Pre-Qualified: | Yes ☐ | No ☐ | Letter Attached: | Yes ☐ | | No ☐ | |
| Pre-Approved: | Yes ☐ | No ☐ | Letter Attached: | Yes ☐ | | No ☐ | |
| Contingencies: | ☐ Need to Sell First | ☐ Engineering Report | ☐ Gift | Other: | | | |
| Comments: | | | | | | | |

**Figure 7.1.** Submit offer.

think of it as an engagement, not a wedding. It's enough of a commitment on both sides that each of you can feel comfortable allocating time and money toward the ultimate contract. You *could* still get burned . . . but if you are, you'll have some recourse.

Most real estate transactions involve standard, boilerplate submit offers. Still, we're talking about people, and egos, and the real world. So you want to stay on top of the process. Talk to your lawyers *every day*. Make sure they're doing what *you* want, not what they want.

## Act II: The Experts

Now things get complicated. Because it's time to bring in the experts—all those folks who will double-check your deal, and double-check each other, then triple-check the same deal and the same others, and then, *maybe*, give their approval. Sort of.

First up (no surprise here!): money. If you'll be working with a mortgage broker, it's time to find her, hire her, and put her to work. (See Chapter 8 for more about these pros.) If you'll be doing the mortgage legwork yourself, get started.

When you and your broker(s) and your bank(s) have done the mortgage dance, and everyone is happy, the financier will hand you a commitment letter: "We agree to give $___ to ____ at _____ terms."

Now more experts come in. The title company will be put to work doing a title search. Your bank will bring in an appraiser and perhaps an engineer to evaluate the deal from all sides. (The bank will hire these folks, then tack their fees onto your closing costs.) You may wish to bring in your own appraiser, and/or your own engineer, to offer further opinions. If so, you'll do the hiring and the paying.

At any moment, any one of these experts may spot a problem. Truth be told, I've never been part of or even *heard of* a real estate deal that didn't involve a problem (or 50). Every such issue can lead to changes in your ultimate deal. So you'll need to remain in close contact with your attorneys.

---

### When You're the Seller

- Have you sent letters notifying all your tenants?
- Have you dealt with all the utility companies you work with?

---

- Have you obtained a certificate of **estoppel** from your commercial tenants?
- Have you made arrangements for any outstanding rent?
- Have you canceled your insurance policies?

**estoppel:** The prevention of a person's asserting a legal right because of prior actions inconsistent with the assertion.

### Act III: The Walk-Through

The day before the closing—or better, on even the day of the closing—walk through the property. I sometimes send an employee of mine to do the walk-through while I'm driving to the closing.

Why? You want to know that the building is still there, and in the condition you're expecting. Maybe there was a fire the night before. Maybe vandals stopped by and broke half the windows. *You never know.* Walk through the property.

It's a wise idea to bring along a digital or Polaroid camera—one that lets you develop the pictures right away. At the least, you want to take notes of any damage or problems you find. Bring whatever you find—notes, pictures—to the closing itself.

Once you're there, in the room, you can present your evidence to the sellers. "Look at this," you'll say. "This is unacceptable." You've just put yourself into a very strong position to negotiate the price downward to cover any repairs you'll have to make. Because chances are, the sellers are packed up and ready to move; they've got the car outside loaded with all their worldly goods. They're not about to argue if you ask for a price reduction—especially not if you've got photos or other evidence in front of you.

### Denouement: The Closing

The day before your closing, your attorney will call or fax you: "This is the money you have to bring to the table." If you don't have a check in your hands at this point, get one.

The closing itself is (hopefully) a bit of an anticlimax—if not downright boring. Bring your pen, and bring something to eat. Because it's *sign, sign, sign*. Break. *Sign, sign*.

Stupefying as all this is, it's what you want. A deal *can* fall through at the closing table itself. It's rare, but it happens. *It's not over till it's over.*

When it's over, don't forget the keys. And the champagne.

# Action Points: Emotions versus Facts

The closing process, from start to finish, involves whole roomfuls of people and—critically important—their egos. This includes you and your own ego.

Remember the conversation we had back in Chapter 4, about commitment? Now is the time to you need to start living that out. It can be so easy for investors to get upset or angry about a deal. *Hell yes, I get upset!* they say to themselves. *C'mon, I've got my career, my reputation, my self-confidence on the line, not to mention my money and my future.* Big stuff. Emotional stuff. *Risky* stuff. I've seen way too many investor hopefuls become so emotionally involved in a deal that they ended up saying, "You know what? Screw you. I'm outta here." And they stalked out.

These folks traded a single moment of satisfaction for a deal that could've set them up for life.

Don't do this. Stay focused. Stay committed. Keep your eyes on the big picture. Remind yourself: *I'm making money here. I can let go of my ego.* Then do it.

Let's practice.

1. Think back to moments in the recent past when you were angry. Really angry. Memorably angry. Now, this could be sweeping righteous anger (*How* dare *you endanger my child?*) or it could be stunningly petty stuff (*How* dare *you overcook my Happy Burger?*). Doesn't matter. Point is, it got to you. **Make a list of your three most recent run-ins with big-time rage.** Try to summarize each incident in a single sentence.
   Situation #1: _____.
   Situation #2: _____.
   Situation #3: _____.
2. Let's look more closely at each incident. What were the actual *facts*? **List at least three facts about each situation** that everyone involved— you, anyone you were angry at, any objective bystanders who might

have witnessed the scene—would all agree on.

Situation #1:

    Fact 1 _____.

    Fact 2 _____.

    Fact 3 _____.

Situation #2:

    Fact 1 _____.

    Fact 2 _____.

    Fact 3 _____.

Situation #3:

    Fact 1 _____.

    Fact 2 _____.

    Fact 3 _____.

3. Now, here's a truth about anger: If you dig deep enough into it, you'll find fear down there. Yep, fear. It may not be obvious right away, but it's there. We get angry when we have something to lose. Maybe it's only a few minutes of time or a little spell of privacy; maybe it's our child, our health, our dignity—or our pride. We get angry when we have something at stake—or think we do.

Look again at your three incidents of anger, and this time dig deeper still. **What was really at stake for you in each case?** What did you stand to lose, or at least *believe* you stood to lose?

Situation #1:

    I stood to lose _____.

Situation #2:

    I stood to lose _____.

Situation #3:

    I stood to lose _____.

4. Reality check time. Take a look at your fears (Step 3) as compared with the facts (Step 2). How well do they match up? **On a scale of 1 through 10, how realistic was your fear in each of the above situations?** That is, if events didn't work out in your favor, would you *really* have lost what you were afraid of losing?

If your anger was directed at a mugger pointing a gun at you . . . well, chances are your fear (*I could lose my life*) was pretty realistic. If, however, you were teed off at the Happy Burger chef (*I could lose my self-respect*)—it might be time to get a grip.

Situation #1:

(completely realistic) 10 9 8 7 6 5 4 3 2 1 (totally delusional)

Situation #2:

(completely realistic) 10 9 8 7 6 5 4 3 2 1 (totally delusional)

Situation #3:

(completely realistic) 10 9 8 7 6 5 4 3 2 1 (totally delusional)

**Now add up these three numbers.** How did you do?

**If your score is 1–10:** Anytime something goes wrong, you feel threatened. Your pride, your self-image, your identity are at stake with every move you make: *If I don't win everything*—you say to yourself—*I must be a loser*. You're not controlling your fears, my friend. They're controlling you.

**If your score is 11–20:** You've got both feet planted in the real world—but you've still got some work to do. *I don't mind losing a battle or two*—you say to yourself—*as long as I win the war*. The higher the stakes, the greater the danger you'll let your emotions overwhelm you.

**If your score is 21–30:** You've got a firm grip on this reality-thing. *Win?*—you say—*Win* what? *We're all just trying to do our best*. If you could bottle your attitude, you'd be a millionaire even *without* this book.

◆ ◆ ◆

Whenever your emotions are out of proportion to the facts, you are suffering from ego. *The fastest way to sabotage your investment career is to lose control of your ego.* And it's one of the easiest, too. I've seen it happen over and over. Investors are so afraid of *losing* that they end up—well, losing. They lose their composure, lose their temper, lose their professionalism, and all too often that means losing out on the deal they want.

If you find yourself getting angry in the midst of a closing—or at any time in your real estate career—stop. Take a moment to pause, breathe deeply, and ask yourself: *What are the facts? What am I afraid of? Do my fears match the facts?* Once you've got a handle on your emotions, you can step back into the fray and act like a winner again.

# 8

# Your Team

There's a big difference between doing something alone and having a team. When you begin your investment career, you're probably not going to have a lot of money to hire people. As you build your investments, however, your team becomes crucial. Although real estate *is* property, it's all *about* people.

There are many benefits—and sometimes a few drawbacks—to tapping into professional expertise along every step of your real estate journey. Let's take a look at these, starting with a brief overview of the team you'll soon be starting to assemble for yourself.

## The Infield: Your "Office"

Your in-house team comprises those professionals who'll help you deal with deals—your money people:

- Scouts
- Real estate brokers

- Mortgage brokers
- Lenders
- Bankers
- Attorneys
- Engineers
- Appraisers
- CPAs
- Bookkeepers

# The Outfield: In the Market

Once you've got investment properties under your wing, you're going to need people to help you take care of them. These include the following:

- Supers
- Maintenance staff
- Plumbers
- Electricians
- Pest control experts
- General contractors
- Management companies

# The Finders

There's no substitute for pounding the pavement of your niche neighborhood yourself, in person, seeing and hearing its culture and ambience, talking to its people, sampling its cuisine, perusing the notices posted on community bulletin boards, attending its events and open houses—*being there*. You'll never get so advanced in your real estate career that *being there* doesn't matter anymore.

But you can't be everywhere, and in particular you can't always be *where the deals are* right when you need to be. That's why your team needs finders—people who can sniff out the deals for you.

### Scouts

I've always used **scouts** (also called **bird dogs**) to help me locate great properties and hot deals. What's a scout, you ask? It's an informal, self-bestowed designation, for starters; you don't go to college and major in Real Estate Scouting. Scouts are the people on the scene, on the streets, hanging out in the neighborhood with an eye toward deals. You'll see them sitting on the front steps and the park benches with the older retired folks, passing a beer back and forth. Talking. Listening. Finding out who's who; who's moving, who's dying, who's having a baby, who's getting a divorce or a new job . . . Scouts are usually young, aggressive, and hungry. They don't have the resources to do the investing themselves, but they want to be in on the action, and they'll do what it takes to find you the deal you want. If a property is about to go on the market—or if there's the slightest chance it might go on the market soon—a scout will be all over it. If Johnny Junior is the owner of record but he'll only sell after Johnny Senior approves—your scout will know that, too. He'll know the discount deals, the bargain deals, the hidden deals, the potential deals. All of 'em.

> **scout:** Also called a **bird dog**, a scout is the person who sniffs out the great deals and inside information real estate investors need. The designation is informal.

How do you find a scout? You don't. Scouts find you. They want your patronage, and the instant they sense you're in the market for opportunities, they'll seek you out. They'll see you in the neighborhood or (more often) at real estate meetings, clubs, seminars, breakfasts, and other events. They'll hand you a business card—which will say "consultant" or "adviser" or "analyst," by the way, and *not* "broker." Scouts are wheelers and dealers, and they don't want the limitations that come trying to operate under a brokerage umbrella.

And by the way, scouts will wheel and deal with you, too, when it comes to getting paid for their services. This is often done as a percentage of the deal price or as a flat fee—but there's no set fee, no set percentage, no set procedure to follow. So negotiate. Wheel and deal yourself. I've had some of the most fun of my life hanging out and (especially) bargaining with the scouts I use. Some are energetic and assertive; others are manic and shameless. They're all . . . interesting. You'll never have a dull moment talking to your scouts, I promise you.

### *Brokers*

Ninety percent of the real estate brokers I've worked with have wasted my time.

Don't get me wrong. Brokers are *wonderful* when they're good. I have a broker in New Jersey who seems to have some kind of direct pipeline into my brain. She knows exactly which properties I'll like, and which ones I won't, and which I'll end up rejecting but really want to check out for myself anyway. She doesn't think about her own commission; she thinks about my company, my interests, my needs, and because of that she gets all my Jersey business.

The problem, though, is that almost anyone can become a broker. You have to take a course (that's way too brief), and then a test (that's way too easy). And remember, brokers don't get paid until they make a sale. Be very careful about the advice they give you. Many of them—not all, but many—will advise you to make deals in *their own* best interests, not yours.

## Show Me the Money

If you don't know this already, you're going to learn it fast: There exists a vast and dizzying array of people out there just panting to hand you money.

Really. So who *are* these folks? And how do you find them? Let's take a look.

### *The Mortgage Broker*

The mortgage broker is the one who finds your money tree. She does the legwork—going to the lenders, getting their specifics, doing the comparisons, making recommendations. In return, she receives a fee of 1 to 2 points.

> **point:** One percent of the total mortgage.

I highly recommend using mortgage brokers. As a real estate investor, you've got a lot on your plate; you just don't have time to go to every bank, every financier. A good broker, on the other hand, already has the connections, the knowledge, and the smarts to find you exactly the program you need. If you're looking at a million-dollar property and hoping to put 10 percent down, for instance, a good broker will tell you right off not to waste your time talking to Citibank or Washington Mutual (for example); these banks aren't interested in 10 percent deals. A good broker will instead steer you to other institutions—maybe smaller banks in Florida, or California—that would love your business. A really good broker will already have close working relationships with individual bankers she can introduce you to.

All of this is what she's paid for, and in my opinion it's worth it. By the way, most brokers are paid by the bank, not you. Even if you have to pay her yourself, though, do it, and be generous.

---

## Choosing a Mortgage Broker

Mortgage brokerage is a hot career right now. There are a lot of brokers out there, and there's a lot of competition among them. So how do you find the right one for you?

Here's what I do. Number one on my own list is that I want a broker who returns my calls. Sounds pretty basic—and it is—but it rules out a huge number of the brokers you're going to contact right off the bat.

I want a broker who really knows the job, and really loves it. Hey, I know my job, and I love what I do. I demand the same from everyone I work with.

I also want someone who specializes in the particular kind of mortgage I need. If I'm buying a million-dollar property, I need a broker who's familiar and comfortable with million-dollar mortgages—*not* someone whose specialty is studios and one-bedrooms. If I'm putting together a new-construction deal, my broker should have a long list of construction loans on her or his résumé.

A final point—and it's important: When I need a broker, I put in calls to three, four, even five of them at the same time. "Here's what I'm looking at," I say. "I'm already talking to Broker A, and Broker B, and Broker C. Tell me, what's the best deal *you* can get me?" I often end up with the same broker—I'm a very big fan of his, because he's proven himself for me over and over again. But I also put in the calls, every time.

Your broker is going to investigate a number of money sources. First on the list—no surprise here—is the bank.

### The Bank

Banks are great. Why? Because the interest rates they charge for loans are going to be the lowest on the market. The downside, however, is that banks generally require a lo-o-o-ong time to close.

> ### Insider's Tip!
>
> Banks will tell you, "Of course we can close in 30 days." I've never seen it happen. It's a big process, and a lot of paperwork needs to be put together. In the beginning, anticipate a closing date that's more like 45 to 90 days away.

### Private Money

Your broker can also introduce you to private money.

John Q. Citizen, for instance, is a businessman who says, "Here, look, I've got $100K I want to lend you. In return, you register the mortgage under my name and pay me 10 percent interest."

The advantage here—and it's can be a huge one—is that Mr. Citizen can close very quickly.

There are two downsides, though. You've already spotted the first one, I'm sure: This loan is more expensive than one you'd get from a bank.

Also, you need to realize that private money may not be reliable. You might spend a lot of time and energy setting up your deal with Mr. Citizen, only to have him call you one night and say, "Well, listen, I just spoke with Mrs. Citizen, and we've changed our minds. We're not going to give you the money." You could be in trouble here—not only is your deal off, but you could lose any down payment you've made.

Save yourself the heartache by using private lenders whom you know well, and who've been in this business for a long time.

> ### Insider's Tip!
>
> Once you have private money in your hands, put it in an **escrow** account until closing, so the lenders cannot change their minds at the last moment.

> **escrow:** An item of value, money, or documents deposited with a third party to be held in reserve until agreed-upon conditions have been fulfilled.

### Hard Money Lenders

Yeah, yeah, I know what you're thinking, but it's not true. Hard money lenders are *not* two guys named Tony who are going to break your kneecaps if you don't pay. These are serious, legitimate companies that lend you very short-term money.

In return, they will charge you an interest rate that could range from *15 to 25 percent* a year. (Yes, you read that right!)

So why on earth would you use them? Because they can close in a week. Think about it. Suppose you run across a brownstone on the Upper East Side that was seriously damaged in a fire 10 days ago. The owners are so desperate to unload it, they'll take $1 million for it—and you know this place is worth at least 10 times that much.

But you've got to close in a week. If you don't have $1 million price tag for the building, and another $1 million for renovations, within that week, this once-in-a-lifetime deal will fall through.

Are you going to turn to a bank, or to private money, in a situation like this? Please say *no* as loud as you can. You are going to go to the hard money lenders.

After you borrow their $2 million, buy the property, renovate it, then turn around six months later and sell it for $8 million—are you going to care that you paid 22, 25 percent in interest? I don't think so.

But this is the only kind of situation in which you should use hard money lenders—when speed is of the essence, and there's no question you can do a flip and turn the property around fast. Don't even consider these lenders for other deals. Given the price tag, the numbers just won't add up.

Your broker might be able to put you in touch with hard money lenders; you can also go on the Internet and do a search under "short-term lending."

## Professional Services

Along with the bankers who give you money, you need bankers whom you give your money *to*—the folks in charge of your business accounts.

And the first thing to know is that you do your banking with a person, not an institution. Find a bank, a branch, and—most important—an individual banker you really like. Then create a relationship. You want your banker to remember your name, your needs, your history. You want a banker who sends birthday cards to your children.

I work with a woman named Susan, who takes care of me like my own mother. Whenever I need some banking help—clearing a check, getting a signature, what have you—I give her a call. Suddenly a process that would normally take three business days takes about three business minutes. Now, I have close to 30 accounts with Susan, so it's definitely worth her while to take my calls. Still, she goes far above and beyond the call for me. Susan's intervention has allowed me to close on properties I would otherwise have missed. She does this for me because my business and my needs matter to her.

---

### Finding Your Team: What You Need to Know

As you work with and interview potential team members, you need to find out the following:

- *Do you know real estate? What other real estate ventures do you work with?* Get a list of past and current real estate clients whom you can contact for references.
- *Do you know entrepreneurs? Are you comfortable with the freewheeling atmosphere of a new business venture? What other start-up ventures have you worked with?* Get a list.
- *Do you own investment properties? What kind? How many?* Get a list.
- *Do you know my niche? Are you comfortable with the needs and culture of the people I serve?*

---

You need the same kind of personal attention from all your professional service people—your lawyers, your accountants and bookkeepers, your appraisers and engineers, the expediters who run interference for you at city hall, the whiz kids who keep your computers running. All of these folks are working for you, and it's worth your while to find the right ones. You want pros who understand your business, know your needs, share your working style, and just plain get along with you.

## Your Team

How do you find them? You devote energy and attention to the task. I've heard it said that the greatest asset you can have in a real estate career is a really good phone book—and I agree. Fill your notebook with the names and numbers of everyone you meet. (See "Assembling Your Team" at the end of this chapter.) Get the business cards of everyone you talk to at real estate meetings. Whenever I teach a seminar, I begin by inviting all my students to pass out their cards; it's a fantastic networking opportunity. Don't stop there, either. If you go to a party, make a point of getting the cards of two or three professionals whose services you might need. Go to the gym and find out what profession the man on the next exercise bike is in—if you could use him, get his card! Go to a family reunion and see if you can learn what all your second and third cousins are up to these days—and what their friends are up to, and their friends' friends. "Oh, your son's opening a restaurant? Tell me, who's his lawyer? Is she any good?" "So you're an architect! Can I ask, who does your books? Do you like him?" Everywhere you go, everything you do, everyone you meet, look for new professional contacts.

Then call these folks and give them a try. You might need to be patient here, because building a great team can take some time. You simply won't mesh with every professional you meet. If you feel at all uncomfortable with or slighted by anyone you work with, move on. You and the venture you're growing deserve the best.

---

### The E-Network

Whenever I hold an open house on one of my properties, I ask the people who visit to sign in with their names and e-mail address. Then the next time I have an apartment with no fee available, I send out a group e-mail to my mailing list. Sure, some people tell me, "Please stop sending me stuff." That's no problem—I just take them off my list. But then there are folks who tell me, "Listen, I found a place for myself, I'm not looking anymore. But my ex-roommate is looking out for a home. I'm going to give him your e-mail."

Every little connection you make could pay off somewhere down the line. So make it!

---

# Property Services

You've heard it before: Good relationships need work. That applies to your marriage, your kids, your in-house investment team . . . and it applies to your properties, too.

No one has yet invented a building that takes care of itself. Buildings need time and attention and, yes, love. And you, my investor friend—you who are busy hustling and talking and living and dying deals—may not have any of those to spare.

That's where your really good phone book comes in once again. You need a Rolodex full of plumbers, carpenters, electricians, pest controllers, glaziers, drywallers, landscapers, painters, trash haulers, carpet layers, tree surgeons, and chimney sweeps. You may, I am told, even need a hydro-fracker. (Just don't ask me why.)

You find these people the same way you found your professional service providers: by looking for them, everywhere you go. Ask everyone you meet about the skilled laborers and craftspeople they've worked with. Ask friends, family, colleagues, acquaintances, wait staff, whomever. Pretty much every man and woman on the street has a story to tell about a contractor, good or bad. Seek these stories out. Save them up. The more names and numbers you can get, the better equipped you'll be when an emergency arises.

If you work with a property management company or with a super (see Chapter 6), a lot of maintenance and repair issues will be dealt with long before reaching your attention; that's why you use these folks. Still, no matter who does your day-to-day building management, keep a phone book full of names anyway. Because you never know.

Your phone book should include the names of backup management companies and supers, too, by the way. You really do never know.

---

### How to Choose a Management Company

The management company you select will serve as your representative to the public—your tenants, your service providers, and so on. So it's crucial to choose the right one, and you must be very careful. No matter how good it is, a management company will never care as much about your property as you do.

---

Here's one thing that could go wrong. If you own a five-family property, you'll probably be looking for a small to medium-sized rental company. So let's say you find a great one—it runs 5,000 apartments, and of those units only three are currently unrented. Well, this company's portfolio looks incredible—a vacancy rate of less than 1 percent. But what if all three of those vacancies are in your building? That's more than half your income you'll be forgoing. You'll be operating in the red. All while working with a company that *on paper* looks fantastic.

So how *do* you choose the right company?

First of all, you choose your management face-to-face. Go and meet them.

Then, at the meeting, you want to ask: "Can I see some of your properties?"

If they reply, "Sure! Stop by next Tuesday at four o'clock . . ."—this is *not* the right company for you. They'll probably be sending someone over at three thirty to clean the buildings.

What you want to hear is, "Sure! Let's go right now."

Another point: Ask for the addresses of several different properties that the company manages. Then go visit these buildings on your own at various hours of the day. You should find yourself locked out—that's what you want. An unlocked front door may be due to negligence. This could be a less-than-attentive management firm.

Request the names and addresses of the other landlords whom the company represents. Call them up and ask questions.

Finally, talk to the tenants living at the properties. Ask how they feel the building is maintained.

Property management is both a huge expense and a critical public relations tool. If you can't do it yourself, be sure to get it right from the start!

## It's Good to Be King

If you were able to finance your investment properties all on your own—through home equity, through savings, through what have you—that's *great*. You've started an empire, and you're in total charge.

Or at least you're in charge *for now*. (So don't skip the rest of this section!)

For most of us, however, our investors are an absolutely critical part of the team. And whether that's you right now or not, it's very likely that as you continue delving into the world of real estate, you'll find yourself relying on investors more and more. There are deals you can do on your own, yes. For the most interesting ones, though—and the ones with the most financial potential—you'll need, and want, a set of investors behind you.

It's important to recognize the difference between *hands-on* investors and *hands-off*—and to do so from the very first moment of your real estate partnership. Hands-off investors may only need a quarterly report to keep them happy. Hands-on investors, on the other hand, might bring their own expertise and connections to the deal, and may want more reward for those efforts. Whatever your relationship, there should never be any ambiguity between you and your investors; be sure the roles are crystal clear from the beginning.

There is no set formula when it comes to paying your investors, although I discuss a few possible arrangements in the sidebar. What really matters here, though, is that you be generous to the people who've given you money. And be especially generous in the beginning. Yes, just at the moment when letting go of your hard-earned money may be most wrenching—that's the moment you really have to do it. Right away, give your investors the biggest return on their money that you can.

---

### First Things First

When it comes to my investors—the people who trusted me with their money back when I was just starting out—my attitude is this: I'd rather lose my money than my investors' money. They come first.

Why? Because they'll brag. They'll show off. ("Oh, my new BMW? Isn't she a beauty! I gave my money to So-and-So, and you should see the return he pays! We're putting a pool in next month, too. Here, let me give you So-and-So's number.") They'll be proud of the money you've earned them. And they'll reinvest with you. For that matter, so will a lot of the people they talk to. Word

---

of mouth from your current investors is the best possible way to attract new ones—rich ones—supportive and generous ones who are all but begging to hand you their money.

## Giving It Back: A Few Thoughts on Investment Return

Consider your investors: Why are they investing in you? What are their expectations? What's their investment history?

Has your cousin's friend's neighbor decided to trust you with her savings, rather than putting them into a CD that pays 1 or 2 percent? Is this her first step into the world of entrepreneurial risk and unsecured loans? Would losing her investment mean her son might have to settle for community college, not the Ivy League? That's one set of considerations for you.

But a millionaire investor might have a whole different perspective. He might be choosing to invest in your property rather than in a portfolio that's historically brought him a 12 percent return. He might be expecting to see dividends and detailed financial analyses within the first few months. He might have lost—and gained—and relost, and regained—a few million dollars over the years in ventures much like yours.

These two investors have very different needs and expectations. The millionaire who's bankrolling almost your entire property might assume, even demand, an arrangement known as 90–10–50–50: He puts in 90 percent, you contribute 10 percent and take out a mortgage in your name; the two of you become 50–50 partners. And given this man's savvy, his huge contribution, his assumption of risk, and his history of success, such an arrangement may very well be worth your while.

The friend-of-a-friend-of-a-friend who gave you $20K, however, might be happy—she might even prefer—to take a much smaller return in exchange for less risk. She might fully expect to wait two or three years for her returns to start coming in. You wouldn't offer her 50 percent when she'd be thrilled to receive 5.

All these factors will come into play as you walk that fine line between offering too much return and offering too little. If you have a choice, though, I'll say it again: Be generous. Generosity is never wasted.

## Taking Care of Your Team

Team building doesn't stop once you've assembled your team. It goes on throughout your career.

Take care of the people who take care of you. You've got a Rolodex full of service providers—so stay in touch with them. Check in now and then, whether that's via phone call, e-mail, newsletter, birthday card, what have you. Remind them of who you are and what you're doing. Even more important, remind yourself of who *they* are and what *they're* up to. You want to know that everyone you depend on will return your calls when you're in a pinch. Keep in touch, give some attention to your team members, and they'll be receptive and ready to help you when it matters most.

Just as important: Pay them well. Don't be stingy. You specialize in what you do best; let them specialize in their jobs, and let them know you appreciate it.

# Action Points: Assembling Your Team

The time to start building your team is now. Make a copy of these pages, then drop everything else you may be doing and promise me you won't read one more word of this book until you've filled in at least two pages' worth of contacts. Carry copies of these sheets with you everywhere you go from now on—I mean every minute of every day—and add more contacts as often as possible.

Name: _____  Role: _____
Phone: _____  E-mail: _____
Notes: _____
_____

## Your Team

Name: _____   Role: _____
Phone: _____   E-mail:_____
Notes: _____
_____

Name: _____   Role: _____
Phone: _____   E-mail:_____
Notes: _____
_____

Name: _____   Role: _____
Phone: _____   E-mail:_____
Notes: _____
_____

Name: _____   Role: _____
Phone: _____   E-mail:_____
Notes: _____
_____

Name: _____   Role: _____
Phone: _____   E-mail:_____
Notes: _____
_____

Name: _____   Role: _____
Phone: _____   E-mail:_____
Notes: _____
_____

Name: _____   Role: _____
Phone: _____   E-mail:_____
Notes: _____
_____

# 9

# Maintain Your Success

Real estate is now your career—your passion—your life. But it's also your job.

And any job can lose its luster over time. Whether you're acting on the Broadway stage, or lunching with power brokers, or playing the PGA circuit, when you do the same thing again and again it's bound to grow stale. That's just the nature of routine.

In real estate, however, that staleness is risky. You don't ever want to lose your edge, or your commitment. So how do you keep this new life fresh? How do you maintain your inspiration, your passion, your nerve?

That's what this chapter is about.

## Recharge Your Batteries

As I've reminded you throughout this book, real estate is a long-term investment. If you're driving on a road trip, it's natural to get sleepy at the wheel. You've got to stop, recharge, reorganize, revisit all the benchmarks you've already passed, and *then* reenter the fray.

Recharging takes on particular importance every time you reach a new level—and reaching new levels is something that'll happen naturally as you continue moving forward in your real estate pursuits. You'll buy one property, two properties . . . and even if all these purchases are of similar value, you will quickly reach more sophisticated levels of bank and investor financing. After a few properties, you may be handling mortgage concerns with several banks. You may have to farm out management issues. You'll simply grow more comfortable with your new role, and your real estate savvy will grow by leaps and bounds, too.

Now we're talking about being a true entrepreneur, the kind with your name written on the office awning. But you can't get there without infusions of outside knowledge.

## A Lifetime of Learning

One of the greatest assets an investor can have is plain old curiosity. Anytime you need a refresher course in this, just take a look at your basic three-year-old: *What's this? What's that? Lemme see! What are you doing? What's this?*

Become (or continue to be) a student of life. Keep growing. Keep sniffing out seminars, books, tapes, whatever you can find. Grab every opportunity that comes along to learn more: Read more complicated articles, a wider variety of books. Take courses in cash-flow analysis and finance issues. Keep up with the financial press to learn more about fluctuating mortgage rates, changing tax laws, and how all of it affects your growing business.

It's all about developing your entrepreneur mind, even more than your real estate mind (you already mastered the real estate mind in Chapters 1 through 8). You're now a *business owner*—yes, you specialize in real estate, but you're a business owner nonetheless. And I can tell you from experience, there's nothing in the world that doesn't in some way connect to your business. You just have to be curious.

## Network, Network, Network

Find or create a network of like-minded individuals so you can bounce your ideas, your inspirations, your hopes and fears off one another. The bigger you become, the more you'll want to spend time with people who can pass on to you the lessons they've learned—*before* you make the same errors! Surround yourself with people who are as powerful as you are.

It's not about having friends who are as rich as you. People have different styles, different professions, different values, different ways of expressing their souls and creativity. The point is to be sure the people in your life are *up to something*. Great minds really do think alike. You may hear a story from a colleague who owns a gym that will give you a whole different perspective on how you manage your real estate team. Business people will encourage you to take risks—that's what they do in *their* professional lives. All these success stories—*everyone's* success story—will recharge you when things aren't going well.

I'm lucky enough to live in New York City, which is chock-full of networking possibilities—you can hardly swing a briefcase in this town without running into a real estate event. Still, wherever you live—Cleveland, Fort Lauderdale, Austin, East Podunk, doesn't matter—you can find opportunities. Look for real estate breakfasts, business seminars, financial meetings, and bring a big stack of business cards. Be visible in your community. *What's this? Where's the real estate in that? Lemme see!*

> ### Insider's Tip!
>
> Banks may be reluctant to give you a mortgage if you already have a high debt-to-income ratio—if, for example, you are investing in many properties with many mortgages. As you move forward in your career, you may want to look for smaller banks that are willing to examine your entire story, not just your numbers.

### *Review Your Five-Year Dream*

Every time you need some recharging, return to your Five-Year Dream. Where are you on this timeline? How close are you to meeting the goals you set for yourself? Are you ahead of yourself, or behind? How can you get back on track, or stay there? Be sure to update your dream often so that it remains ahead of your personal growth curve, and continues to inspire you as much as it did in the beginning.

I lost track of my own Five-Year Dream . . . but in a good way. When I purchased my first property, I had a clear picture of my immediate future:

*Every two to three years, I will buy a property, exactly the same type.* Then suddenly, after two years, I looked around and realized that I owned 18 buildings. There were also new activities: I bought **lots**, flipped lots. My two-year-old dream had become obsolete and irrelevant. So I had to adjust it— although this time, I was able to include goals I'd previously never even heard of!

> **lot:** Raw land; a piece of undeveloped land.

As you learn and network and grow and buy and sell and deal, you'll want to adjust your own five-year picture, too. Be sure you always have something concrete to aspire to. I promise you, you'll never run out of dream.

### Make Your Workspace Work for You

I am lucky enough to have an office now, because I'm completely full-time. In the beginning, I worked from a desk in the corner of our bedroom. If that's you, don't worry—you can do world-class work from any workspace in the world.

Still, your space should be part of your motivation. Create a professional environment for yourself—one that inspires you. Surround yourself with images that remind you of your dreams. I have a framed photo of my first property on the wall; a fellow investor put up an enlarged copy of the first check she received from her first tenant. One of my seminar students put up some framed Monopoly money. He said, "It's a picture of my dream." What ideas do you have to create a picture of your own dream? Do it!

Keep your space organized, and reserve it for work and work alone. You want your office to be imbued with an atmosphere of professionalism, not leisure. The space should allow you to step into your business future; it should truly call you to be great—to be productive and sharp. If you simply must play computer games, or surf the Web for sports news or shoe bargains, or pursue leisure reading or TV, *don't do it in your workspace*. Do it somewhere else. Simply the act of sitting down at your desk should focus your mind on work.

If that desk is sitting in a corner of your living room, or in a converted closet—no problem. It's still the arena where your dreams come true. No matter how small or humble the space, your real estate career can flourish there.

And when you're ready to move into an office with your name on the awning—hey, do it! Just keep the new space as focused, as sharp, as organized, and as professional as that humble desk.

### Look the Part, Act the Part, Be the Part

I used to wonder why people spend money on clothes to work out in. It takes maybe three minutes before these beautiful designer duds are sweaty, grubby—all but ruined. Why bother?

Then I started working out myself, and right away, I got it. There is just something about donning sharp, specialized clothing that says to me, *Let's do it! Time to rock!*

I was an actor for many years. And the same thing used to happen to me before I took the stage: Donning the costume focused me. Looking the role *is* being the role. They're tied up together, inextricably.

As a real estate entrepreneur, you too have got to walk the walk and talk the talk—and dress them both. It's time to get professional. Remember what Mom told you when you started your first job: "Don't dress for the job you have; dress for the job you want"? Well, once again, Mom was right. (Admit it: She was dead-on about eating your vegetables, wasn't she?) You're an investor now, so look like one. It'll make more difference than you can imagine. (But wait on the Mercedes until you see the big cash flow.)

Do not forget a pocketful of business cards that proclaim your new title!

Another critical part of your image—your real estate costume, so to speak—is the portfolio you use to introduce yourself and your business. This is the info packet you give out to potential investors, to the professionals you work or network with, to anyone who wants to know more about what you do. If you don't have one yet, it's time to begin the process.

Your portfolio should detail your current investments, including each property, the neighborhood, your previous successful projects, and the background of the facilitator (that's you, and your company). You may want to include letters from past satisfied investors, plus photographs of the property. Adding a summary of what's possible with each property (future development ideas, observations on recent changes to zoning) as well as the risks involved in investing will round out your info packet.

Revisit this portfolio at regular intervals. (Once a month isn't too often!) As your savvy increases—once you're at the level of courting sophisticated investors—you may want to move beyond bare-bones spreadsheet presentations and start creating graphical files. If graphic design isn't your forte, consider hiring a designer or tapping into the expertise of your team members.

---

### A Crucial Warning: Blue-Sky Laws

Please check with an attorney before handing out *any* investment offerings. There are very specific laws concerning private equity investments in the United States.

These regulations are commonly known as "blue-sky laws." (An early-twentieth-century judge—so the story goes—once likened all too many investment ventures as having "as much value as a patch of blue sky.") Specific regulations vary from state to state, but all of them require you to register your investment offerings and provide accurate financial records. To get the details of your state's policies, *talk to your lawyer*.

There are a lot of investment scams out there these days, just as there were a hundred years ago. The hotter the market, the more scams are out there. It's worth your while to distinguish yourself from these fraudsters with full disclosure and legal compliance. Stay aboveboard in all your dealings!

---

### Schedule It

Your work systems must include a schedule. Do not trust yourself to get your real estate work done as the spirit moves you. Get it done as your calendar moves you. You set up a date book for yourself in Chapter 4, and it's critical to keep it up-to-date—and to follow it!

## Staying on Top

The way to stay on the top of your career is (no big surprise here!) to stay on top of your market.

Always know what's happening in your market. Do not fall asleep.

If the market goes up—way up—crazy up—it may be time to refinance or even cash out. When real estate prices are skyrocketing, that's the moment when you want to go back to your bank and say, "Hey, remember that building we own? It's doubled in value. Give me some money." Refinancing lets you pull funds out of your properties—even if you only purchased them a few years ago. Those funds will keep you in the investing forefront.

Or it may be time to sell. I'm not a big fan of selling (keep reading to learn why), but there are times when it's appropriate. It's certainly worth keeping in the back of your mind, as an option.

What happens when the market is going down? As long as you don't sell, a market downturn shouldn't have a big impact on you. If you can maintain a positive cash flow—and you were smart enough to set aside money for a rainy day (you did set aside money for a rainy day, didn't you?)—you should be fine. People always need a place to live. And because you're a good landlord (you are a good landlord, aren't you?), your tenants will want to stay with you.

## When to Refinance? When to Sell?

Here's a quick quiz for you: When should you refinance? When should you sell?

The answers:

1. Always
2. Never

Okay, I'm generalizing. Still, you get my drift.

Why do I love refinancing? You can keep on doing it! Take the equity when you can, and invest in your next property. As long as refinancing does not cause the property's cash flow to turn negative, keep on pulling out the equity to leverage your assets. Don't pull every penny available out of the refinance, however, because if the market takes a downturn, you may have trouble paying the mortgage.

There are only two possible reasons to sell. Number one: If someone offers you an insanely high price for your property—then, yes, at that point you can *think about* selling.

*My very first investment property stayed in my hands for only 14 months. Why? Because at the end of that time, somebody came along and offered me 175 percent of what I'd paid. One hundred and seventy-five percent! No bank in its right mind would have appraised my property for that price in such a short time. You bet I sold, and even after I'd spent weeks in negotiations, and paid the taxes and closing costs, I still made an almost obscene amount of money on the deal.*

The second reason to sell a property is when you'd like to go to the next level. If you're tired of managing single homes and you want to move into multifamily units, or high-rises, you can sell your holdings and begin to create economies of scale. Many investors, for instance (and this includes me), would much rather manage a building of 60 units than manage 60 single-unit homes. With a single building, a single person—you, or a super—can take care of everything. With 60 individual homes, on the other hand, just driving from property to property will require three or four full-time managers, and the cost of cars and fuel.

The economies of scale that such a career change can give you may (just *may*) make selling worth your while.

---

### Buy Assets, Not Liabilities

Assets are the things that make money for you. Liabilities are the things that cost you money—your car, for instance.

And don't get me wrong: Liabilities can be great. Your car, for instance! Still, the money you spend on these items is really money you throw out the window. When you're getting your start in real estate, you need to focus on assets. Stop buying liabilities during this time so that you can build up a portfolio of assets that make you money.

It won't be long until you can take on liabilities again. Three years from now, five years, you'll be able to buy the car you want. You'll be able to afford the vacations, the clothes, the gadgets you want—out of your income from real estate. Your car is a wonder-

---

ful thing, I know, but won't it be even better when you drive it knowing that the property you own is making enough money for you to cover your monthly payments?

Which are—by the way—deductible. Isn't real estate a fine thing?

# Over Your Head

Having available cash doesn't mean it all needs to be spent. As you begin to grow your empire, watch out for two critical pitfalls: overhead and over-leveraging.

### Overhead

When you began your investment career, you did everything yourself. You pored over the literature, you pounded the pavement, you unearthed the deals and the tenants. You may have even swung the sledgehammer and unclogged the toilets.

Then, as you got bigger and bigger, and your investment career grew and grew, you realized you needed help. And so you started to outsource. Pretty soon you had a part-time assistant, who then evolved into full-time. Then you found team members to do the things you're not so good at, allowing you to focus on what you do best—whether finding the deals, maintaining relationships with investors, or installing the plumbing.

This is all good, but it's risky, too. Because if you're not careful, here's what will happen: You'll wake up one morning and realize that your overhead has shot up 200, 400, even 800 percent—but your profits haven't.

To avoid this, build your team slowly, over time. You didn't build your real estate portfolio in a day or two (at least I hope you didn't!); your team should evolve just as gradually and deliberately. Be sure that you need a new team member before you go out and hire her. Be sure, too, that your cash flow justifies her. You want to have enough money set aside to pay a new employee's salary *before* you hire or even place the want ad. And don't forget to revisit your team's operations frequently to make sure each member brings to the company in profits at least the value of her salary—if not more.

### *Overleveraging*

Once upon a time there lived a cricket and an ant. The cricket spent all summer rubbing her legs together languidly, creating beautiful music as she watched the ant scurry about. "What on earth are you racing for?" asked the cricket from her hammock. "It's summer, for goodness' sakes! Relax and enjoy it a moment!"

"I mustn't," panted the ant. "Soon winter will be upon us, and I have to prepare my stores of food!"

The cricket shrugged and returned to sunning herself.

Six months later, the ant sat safely in his carved-out hill, eating his protected food, while the cricket shivered in the icy cold and wondered, belatedly, where all the food had gone, and when her stomach would stop rumbling.

Markets go up, markets go down. Even when things are going terrifically well, none of us can predict the future. How many people bought tech stocks in the late 1990s, hung on to them for dear life, rode the wave of profits and more profits—and were still hanging on when that wave crashed into the sand? *Let me keep it just one more day!* thought the investors as they lay in their hammocks, listening to beautiful music, already counting up the future vacations they'd be taking in the Bahamas. And then . . .

The moral of the story is this: When the market is going gangbusters, *watch out*. If you keep buying, and leveraging, and buying, and leveraging—well, yes, you *might* be able to eke out a little more money. Or you might not. It's not worth the risk.

Leverage is a good thing—*when it's handled responsibly*. Step back often and reevaluate your position. Never let overleverage leave you out in the cold.

## The Value of Your Name

As you build your career you want to build your reputation, too—and you want that reputation to be a "Great Landlord."

We live in a small world. Even New York City is, in the end, a small town. Here's what I mean: Everything you do, every action you take, will come back to you. There's no such thing as anonymity. People *will* know your name.

# Maintain Your Success

That name is valuable. It's crucial. Your reputation *is* your business future. If you act like a slumlord, it's going to come back to haunt you. If you act like a fantastic landlord, however, you'll have tenants lined up to live in your properties.

I get a lot of my new tenants when my current tenants give referrals to their friends and family. "You've got to live in this building," they'll say, "my landlord is *great*." It's true, too—I am very proud of the way I treat my clients. I furnish each apartment with flower boxes. I send my tenants a holiday card thanking them for a wonderful year. It doesn't stop there, either. After a complicated closing, I'll send fruit baskets to the offices of my team members—my attorney, my banker, my investors. These are gifts not just for the principals, but for all the staff, too. My lawyer's secretary spends hours on the phone facilitating my deals. My mortgage broker's assistant comes in on Saturdays to help me out. I make a point of knowing all these people—remembering their names and recognizing how much they do for me. I take care of them, and you'd better believe they take care of me.

*Judy, the second-floor tenant in one of my buildings, was a retired woman who loved to garden. I spent a lot of time talking with her—just shooting the breeze as I checked in on my properties. She was a fine person, and I liked her. She must've felt the same, because one day she said to me, "Boaz, the front yard here is very nice. It's clean. But I really want to make it beautiful. Would you mind?"*

*I said, "Sure thing. Whatever you want to buy, go for it."*

*Judy was thrilled, and she put in an enormous amount of work creating a landscaped garden in front of my building. All I had to do was pay for the materials—some plants, some mulch, some tools. My tenant did all the work. The property became a little green wonderland in the middle of the block.*

*Eventually, I sold that property for a huge profit, and Judy's front yard was a big part of the reason why. I know that because the buyer told me so.*

At the same time, of course, you need to know your limits—your time limits and your financial limits. This is a profession that can eat up your life if you're not careful, and whenever it takes too much out of you, you need to step back. Being generous can quickly turn into being overwhelmed. Determine exactly how much time and money you can spend on your work, and stick to it.

# Action Points: Your Name, Your Future

So how can you build a reputation you're proud of? For starters, you do it your way. Just as you determined your real estate niche earlier in this book, now it's time to determine your "generosity niche."

Here's a brainstorming task to help you come up with your own unique methods.

1.  Think about the various people in your professional life—all of them, from your team members to your investors, your financiers, your tenants, your support network, even the folks who deliver your mail. **How do you think each person sees you?**

    Fill in the blanks below with each individual's perspective on you. As always, be as honest as you can.

    Here are some examples to get you started:

    I am known by my accountant to be someone who pays on time.
    I am known by my attorney to be someone who always thinks outside of the box.
    I am known by my customers—my investors—to be someone who returns much more profit than they expected.

    I am known by _____ to be someone who_____.
    I am known by _____ to be someone who_____.
    I am known by _____ to be someone who_____.
    I am known by _____ to be someone who_____.
    I am known by _____ to be someone who_____.
    I am known by _____ to be someone who_____.
    I am known by _____ to be someone who_____.
    I am known by _____ to be someone who_____.

# Maintain Your Success

I am known by _____ to be someone who_____.
I am known by _____ to be someone who_____.
I am known by _____ to be someone who_____.
I am known by _____ to be someone who_____.
I am known by _____ to be someone who_____.
I am known by _____ to be someone who_____.
I am known by _____ to be someone who_____.
I am known by _____ to be someone who_____.
I am known by _____ to be someone who_____.
I am known by _____ to be someone who_____.
I am known by _____ to be someone who_____.
I am known by _____ to be someone who_____.

Each person you come in contact with, on a daily, or weekly, or monthly basis, knows you and has a mental image of you. Think of it as your label—your "brand" (like Sears, or Target, or Microsoft)—your reputation. Every action you take, every word you say, adds to this image—or detracts from it!

Step back often and evaluate how the people in your life see you. Is the label they're seeing the label you hope to project? Are you building for yourself the reputation you want?

2. Your personal label—the value of your personal name—will also lead you to create your mission and vision as a company.

My own mission statement came organically out of the work I was doing in my community:

*At ORE International, we are committed to serving the community by providing solutions to major real estate and housing challenges, and creating wealth for all involved in real estate investment with us while maintaining the highest level of personalized customer service and integrity in our business relationships.*

**What's your company's mission statement?** If you don't have one already, write one now:

## The Real Estate Millionaire

At _____, we are committed to _____

_____

_____

_____

_____

_____

_____

_____

_____.

Post this statement prominently in your workspace. Live with it for a while. Is it complete and appropriate? Does it need to be tweaked? And most important: Are you living it out?

3. Now think about you and your mission from the perspective of each person you listed above. **How can you show these individuals who you are?** How can you live out your mission in your interactions with them?

I can live out my mission with_____ by _____.

I can live out my mission with_____ by _____.

I can live out my mission with_____ by _____.

I can live out my mission with_____ by _____.

I can live out my mission with_____ by _____.

I can live out my mission with_____ by _____.

I can live out my mission with_____ by _____.

I can live out my mission with_____ by _____.

I can live out my mission with_____ by _____.

I can live out my mission with_____ by _____.

I can live out my mission with_____ by _____.

I can live out my mission with_____ by _____.

I can live out my mission with_____ by _____.

I can live out my mission with_____ by _____.

I can live out my mission with_____ by _____.

I can live out my mission with_____ by _____.

I can live out my mission with_____ by _____.

I can live out my mission with_____ by _____.

I can live out my mission with_____ by _____.

# 10

# Now That You're a Millionaire . . .

Beginning with no experience, no contacts, no training in the field, and no cash, I turned a $0 real estate investment into more than a million in less than two years.

How?

## The 22-Month Real Estate Millionaire: How I Made My First Million Dollars

Here's how.

### Enter Deal #1

The first property I purchased was on Brooklyn's Gates Avenue. After I'd looked at 30 properties—and realized none of them would work for me, or even come *close*—a real estate broker led me to a neighborhood called Clinton Hill, which I had never heard of. It was full of new construction. We stopped at a work site on a block of six brick row houses. At this point in my budding investment career, I no longer had qualms about talking to total strangers, so I approached the foreman and asked him about the property. He told me the work was only about half done and gave me the developer's business card. I called that afternoon.

Because this property was so far from finished, it hadn't yet appeared on the radar screen of any Realtors. I was able to purchase it for $369,000. I spent $20,000 renovating, including the addition of another apartment. Now, you need to know that this maneuver isn't always legally possible, but the particular property I bought was already zoned to allow for an addition. Moreover, the renovation didn't require additional heating, air-conditioning, or boilers—all elements that can really complicate a conversion. I simply had a kitchen added and created a loft-style space that would suit my niche, housing for fellow actors.

---

### By the Way . . .

It should not have cost me $20,000 to add an apartment to my property; the price tag should have been closer to $10,000. But I was new to real estate and didn't have a strong network (okay, *any* network) of carpenters, handymen, and construction workers backing me up. This is the kind of mistake many newbie investors make—you can expect to make a lot of them yourself. Just trust that you *will* gain the expertise and the contacts you need over time.

---

I didn't know anything about renovation, so I was on-site every day to watch and learn what the contractors were doing and to be on top of their work. The building was brand-new, so construction was straightforward—no surprise plumbing from 1902 to slow down the work flow.

Because this was a neighborhood in transition, within a year and two months I sold my property for $689,000. After expenses, I netted $300,000 on this deal—not counting the rental income I'd received during the 14 months I owned the house. This income—it was a positive-cash-flow building, of course!—was $16,000.

### On to Deal #2

While I was the owner of Building 1, I purchased several other properties for investors. I still didn't have any capital of my own yet, so I exchanged my time for equity in the properties (sweat equity—you know all about this from Chapter 5). All of these efforts—from Properties 1 and 2—netted me $28,000 in rent during this first year. In the second year, the rent roll jumped to $61,000 because by now I had more units in larger buildings.

I paid most of these profits to my investors in the first year and ended up with $28,000 cash for myself, which was a fortune to me in those days.

### Deal #3

A very interesting property in Union City, New Jersey, allowed me to learn about zoning and subdivision. I bought a building that had nine units, along with an adjacent parking lot. Examining the records, I discovered that although New Jersey has strict rules about how much parking must be provided for each apartment, this particular property was built before the laws were changed, thus allowing our property to be **grandfathered**. Thus, the parking lot could be subdivided from the building.

> **grandfathered:** Protected by previous laws.

I went ahead with this deal despite the fact that the rent roll was low—it was cash-flow positive by 8.1 percent only. I paid $290,000—a great deal considering the nine units. I spent about $30,000 renovating the building, plus about $5,000 in attorney fees to subdivide the lots. I also paid $2,000 to a local architect who already had **rubber-stamp plans** for a three-family house prepared.

> **rubber-stamp plans:** Premade architectural blueprints that can be adjusted to any property with the same lot size.

Then I sold the parking lot—with approved plans—for a net profit of $125,000. Because this money came from the parking lot, I hadn't even included it in my pre-deal cash-on-cash analysis—sheer gift. Someone *else* built that three-family on the lot.

Finally, after three months, I sold the original (now renovated) building for $390,000—a profit of $100K, without even changing the rent roll.

### Deal #4

I purchased a 20-by-100-foot lot for $32,000. The standard lot size in New York is 25 by 100 feet, so this was just a hair smaller. Again, I found an architect who had some preprepared building plans—he simply combed through his files, pulled out a structure he'd designed for a 20-by-100-foot lot, and changed the address written on the blueprints. After four months and with the plans approved, I sold the property for $80,000, leaving me with a net of $45,000.

### Next: Deal #5

A six-family apartment building, plus a store, was almost vacant. I was able to buy this property at a very deep discount because of the tenant problems. Still, I found a willing buyer who was very happy with his end of the deal. I gave him a **contract vendee** and walked away with $85,000 cash. Yes, I had to pay taxes on it, but no transfer taxes.

> **contract vendee:** The designated purchaser of a contract. The term is also used to refer to the arrangement itself.

### Brief Detour: Deal #5A

Deal 5 was the first of two flips that I successfully completed in this same time frame. The second one—Deal 5A—was a parking lot. This lot was zoned M-1 (*M* stands for "manufacture"), but then the municipality made a proposal for a speculative zoning change. The moment I heard about this upcoming change, the lot sold for a $30,000 profit. Total profit on the two flips: $115,000.

### Back to Deal #6

Florida deals caught my attention. After seeing results in my niche on my home turf, I became more open to the idea of spreading my wings a bit, but I still wanted as conservative an investment as I could find.

So I approached a solid builder—among the largest developers in Florida, whose company is traded on the NASDAQ—and I bought in at phase one, preconstruction. I chose the location, did my research, traveled to Florida, and bought a single-family home on the state's western coast for $269,000. I put the house on the market 45 days before it was in move-in condition, and I sold it when construction was complete for $350,000. A local broker found a buyer who was willing to close without my being there—I simply handed over **power of attorney** to my lawyer and profited $75,000 while sitting at home in New York City.

> **power of attorney:** Legal permission for another adult to act on your behalf.

### Finally: Deal #7

I bought a 12-family as a rental property. This building was a complete shell—no one had lived there for 22 years. I gut-renovated the entire building, A to Z, and created a beautiful set of apartments.

Just after the construction was completed, I refinanced the property (now worth $450,000 more!) and held on to it.

During this same stretch of time, I gut-renovated another beautiful brownstone, this one a two-family—I bought, renovated, and refinanced. Together, from these two properties, I pulled out $232,000.

### Adding It All Up

So let's go through the numbers:

1. Conversion of two-family property to three-family: $300,000 profit.
2. Investment property rent rolls: $89,000 ($28,000 the first year, $61,000 the second).
3. A nine-unit property plus parking lot subdivision: $210,000 profit ($100,000 on the building, $110K on the lot).
4. Flipping a 20-by-100-foot lot: $45,000 net profit.
5. Two flips: a six-family house with store, and a parking lot zoned M1: $115,000 profit.
6. Preconstruction deal in Florida: $75,000.
7. Refinances, one of a 12-family, the other of a two-family: $232,000.

The grand total? A million dollars and an extra $66,000 in 22 months.

# Where to Next? Becoming a Mogul–and Beyond

Think back to the Five-Year Dream you created in Chapter 4. Have you fulfilled it? If your goal was to own one property and have a bit of extra cash every month—well, chances are you're there now. And that's great.

But if your dream involved reaching the level of owning 10, 15, maybe 20 properties, and never again asking yourself that ugly question, *Can I afford it?*—you've been dreaming of mogul-dom, my friend, and you may still have a ways to go.

---

### Insider's Tip!

Never look in anyone else's pocket. It will only make you crazy. *Is he getting more money out of this deal than I am? Does she have a bigger percentage than me?* Don't even go there. If it works for you, do it. If it doesn't, don't. Period.

---

So let's return to place where this book began. Why did you want to get into real estate? You've begun the process of creating a future for you and your family to step into; don't stop now (or ever). Be very clear, always, on how your life is going to look when you became a mogul. What's going to be the feeling available to you once you're supporting yourself and your loved ones? Keep this feeling alive and real inside you all the time. Never let go of it.

Remember, too, that the Five-Year Dream you started with may be completely obsolete by now or in the very near future. At this point, you've probably already learned about (or successfully completed!) options you'd never even heard of back then. More and more of these discoveries await you. You'll be reaching level after level *beyond* anything you've ever dreamed of. A lifetime isn't long enough to discover them all.

---

### The Wild Blue Yonder

Whatever you want out of life, you can have. Some people dream about $100,000 a year–*Oh, wouldn't that be great?* they say. Well, these people just put a ceiling over their dreams. *I'll dream*

---

> so *high . . . and no higher.* Is that you? Is that all you ask from your dreams?

So let's talk about those next levels. What are they? How do you find them, and how do you reach them? I can't give you a list of everything that's possible in this huge world of real estate investing, because I don't know it all. No way have I finished this process! Still, I have a few thoughts and directions for you.

I'm done with investing in single buildings. I got my start in these buildings, and they did beautiful things for me, but they're not interesting to me anymore; I need new challenges. So I've branched out now into consulting, into commercial real estate, into partnerships and other sophisticated investment relationships, into teaching, and (you may have noticed this) into books.

As you, too, get restless with what you have and start reaching out for more, consider the following:

- It may be time for you to investigate commercial properties. These are higher-risk investments, heavily affected by the economy; if we happen to hit an economic downturn, you stand to lose a lot. They're not a good place to start a career. By the same token, however, they can make you a lot of money, and they're fascinating, invigorating, exciting projects to work with.
- Look for your next niche. There's not a person in the world who has a single facet and a single facet only; if you're alive, you have innumerable interests, fields of expertise, comfort zones. How can you turn these niches into cash? *Where's the real estate in that?*
- Look at other geographic areas. I've been spending a lot of time learning about the Virginia real estate market—very different from New York City, with different needs, property types, conditions, everything. It's intriguing. Florida is an exciting place to be these days. So is anywhere that baby boomers are retiring. (And do I need to even *mention* the part about business travel to warm climes? In February? That's tax-deductible?)
- Development might be the next stop on your journey. Think about buying land. Or see if you can do what I did—buy an existing property

that happened to include a parcel of raw land right next door (see Deal #3, above). I sold my own piece of land; you might do the same, or you might want to develop the parcel yourself. Like commercial investment, construction can be a very risky direction to go—that also offers the possibility of massive profits and pulse-pounding excitement. (Which maybe your nine-to-five in a cubicle is a little short on, eh?)

What else? Oh, plenty. You have hardly scratched the surface.

## The Feds Take Away . . . and Then They Give Back

The United States Treasury wants to give *you* money. There are a lot of government programs out there designed to help you invest in real estate—well-funded programs designed to help make affordable housing available across the nation. Hook up with the right one of these and you can buy a property with *no* money down, courtesy of Uncle Sam. Check your local Housing and Urban Development (HUD) offices for details on current programs, or visit this agency's Web site: www.hud.gov.

## Profiting from Nonprofits

Another avenue to investigate is not-for-profit organizations, many of which are also deeply involved with housing issues. I deal with an agency, for instance, that works with AIDS patients, in particular hooking them up with affordable housing—which can be very difficult to find for those with overwhelming medical needs and bills. This group has the funds and the client base; what it desperately needs, however, is the actual buildings. That's where I come in. I feel great about taking care of people this way—giving back to the community. And at the same time, I'm supporting my business, too.

Another group I work with focuses on neighborhood renovation. Once you buy a building, the folks at this nonprofit will give you the money and support you need to renovate it. Then they take over the building and rent it from you for 5 to 10 years, while also doing all the maintenance and property repair themselves. Think about it: Once you buy the property, all that's left for you to do is deposit the profits every month.

How do you find programs and groups like these? Check your state's department of social services. To find this, a Web search using the keywords "social services" and your state's name should get you pointed in the right direction.

---

### Don't Change, Adjust

Real estate investment is not a regulated industry, which means that people can do very well, very fast. If you're going to keep up, you may need to be tough with people. Sometimes really tough.

As you continue in your career, you may find yourself discouraged by your own behavior. Remember this: You don't have to change who you are, but you may have to adjust. Look at what you're good at, what your style of negotiating is, your style of management. Then think about how you can adjust this—your skills, your style, your soul—to keep on top of this competitive industry. It can be done. I've met extraordinary investors who are the kindest people in the world. They've simply tweaked their style to give play to their aggressive, rough-and-tumble impulses while they're dealing in the real estate arena.

---

### *Partnerships*

There's comes a point in this real estate world at which you hit a limit and you can go no further—*unless you have partners*. You can make a million dollars on your own, absolutely. You can make a lot more than that, too. But if you want to work at the $100 million level, you've got to create partnerships.

There are as many partnership opportunities and structures out there as there are potential partners. You can set up your working arrangements however you want. And everyone you meet is a potential partner—the woman sitting next to you at an investment seminar, the man across the negotiating table from you as you buy your first property, the corporation trying to outbid you as you buy your seventeenth. They could all be your allies next week.

Ultimately, though, partnership is about *people*—people who share your interests, your career, your risks. People who know exactly how you spend your days and what you worry about in the middle of the night. People there to support you. Real estate is all about people—and I, for one, am forever grateful.

---

### What It's All About

When I bought my first property, I was operating on less than a shoestring. I was broke, I was scared, I was close to overwhelmed. And I knew absolutely nothing about property maintenance. I needed a handyman badly—I needed him *now*—but how on earth could I afford him? Well, I couldn't, so here's what I did. I went to my friend Ron and said, "Here's the deal. I'm going to buy this building. I think it's a great idea. And then I'm going to buy another one, and another one. I don't have any cash to pay you right now, but I want you on my team. If you're along for the ride, and you're involved in what I'm doing, and you believe in me the way that *I* believe in me, I promise you that at the back end you'll have a stake in my company."

Well, Ron is still working with me today. I paid him back over and over again. And yes, he does have a healthy stake in my company.

I'm grateful to him for sharing my dream—without pay!—back when it was just a dream. He allowed me to succeed. But maybe the best part is that Ron is happy, too. "Listen, *you* invested in *me*," he says. "You had faith in *me*."

---

◆ ◆ ◆

One final thought for you: Becoming a mogul means commitment to real estate. Personal sacrifice. You have to give up a lot to make it in this business.

But you don't have to give up your soul. You don't have to give up your moral center. It *is* possible to be a millionaire and still face yourself in the mirror every morning. I know because I've done it. I have a wonderful life, and I still like the man I am.

You have to be tough with people in this job, but there's a big difference between being tough with people and screwing them over. No job, no career, no amount of money is worth giving up your humanity for—so don't. Be tough, be firm, hold people to their promises—even if you need to look like a jerk. Be strong enough to hang on to your decency. Then you'll *really* be a success.

Deep down, my goal was never to be rich; what I've always wanted is to be generous. Knowing that I can make a difference—I can create a better world—truly, that's the greatest reward there is.

# Glossary

**ADA (Americans with Disabilities Act):** A federal civil rights law requiring that (among other things) landlords and employers must make reasonable accommodations to allow the disabled access to facilities.

**application fees:** Fees that must be paid for banking services (such as mortgages) and for local licenses to perform construction.

**appraisal:** A professional opinion of a property's value.

**appreciation:** An increase in value over time.

**asset:** Something of value that is owned.

**assignment:** A documented offer on a property that can be taken over by a third party if the party making the offer so chooses.

**binder check:** A check that binds a deal, generally 1 percent of the purchase price.

bird dog: See *scout*.

capital gain: Profit on the sale of an asset.

capital gains tax: Tax paid on the profit.

carrying costs: Total expenses that must be paid during the period of "no income," which carry you through until income is generated. Prime among carrying cost are the real estate taxes you'll be paying on the lot during the construction process.

collateral: Something of value given as security for a loan.

comp: Short for *comparable*, a comp is a real estate transaction that took place in the same neighborhood, in the same time frame, and for the same type of property as yours. Comparing your deal with similar deals allows an appraiser to determine if the price is appropriate.

compounding: The process of reinvesting interest to earn additional interest. The more frequent the compounding, the more you earn. Compounded interest is paid on both the accumulated interest as well as the original principal.

contract: A legal document spelling out an agreement. It may or may not be assignable, depending on its specific language.

contract vendee: The designated purchaser of a contract. The term is also used to refer to the arrangement itself.

default: Failing to fulfill a legal agreement.

depreciation: The reduction in the value of a property expressed as a deduction for income tax purposes.

down payment: The portion of the full purchase price that is not part of the mortgage.

due diligence: The careful consideration of each aspect of a proposed asset purchase.

equity: The money value of a property.

# Glossary

escrow: An item of value, money, or documents deposited with a third party to be held in reserve until agreed-upon conditions have been fulfilled.

expediter: A real estate professional who specializes in expediting the investment process in the municipality—by obtaining permits, paying fees, removing violations, registering rents, and so on. Your expediter will be your liaison to the local and state municipalities.

flip: Resale of a property immediately following the purchase.

good-faith payment: A dollar amount given by the prospective buyer to the seller that symbolizes a commitment to close the deal. Good-faith payments are common, and they can run anywhere from $100 to $500.

grandfathered: Protected by previous laws.

home equity line of credit (HELOC): A mortgage on your home that operates like revolving credit. You may borrow none, a portion, or all of the available credit based on your needs.

interest: The fee paid for borrowing money.

leverage: Increased power through the use of borrowed money.

liability: Something for which one is liable; an obligation, responsibility, or debt. Examples of liability would include a mortgage payment, an insurance bill, and a tax bill.

lien: A claim against a property. A lien gives a creditor the right to take a property if you don't pay a debt. Liens can be consensual (including mortgages and home equity loans) and nonconsensual (including liens for unpaid taxes and contractors).

lot (n.): Raw land; a piece of undeveloped land.

LTV (loan to value): The relationship in percentages between the loan given (debt) and the total value of the property.

mixed-use: Residential and commercial units in the same building.

# Glossary

**mortgage:** A written agreement that creates a lien against property as security for a debt.

**motivated seller:** Someone who's anxious to sell for any reason—financial, personal, professional, whatever.

**net return:** The amount of money you take in after all your expenses are paid.

**nonrecourse mortgage:** A mortgage in which the bank agrees to lend to a corporation from the very beginning.

**OSHA (Occupational Health and Safety Administration):** A federal agency that creates and enforces business health and safety regulations.

**passive income:** Money you don't have to work for.

**phase one:** The first phase of a project. For a new development, this phase occurs before building begins.

**point:** One percent of the total mortgage.

**power of attorney:** Legal permission for another adult to act on your behalf.

**principal:** The base amount of the loan owed.

**refi:** Real-estate-speak for "refinance."

**refinance:** To reorganize the financing of a property by taking out a new loan.

**rehab:** Short for rehabilitation—the total renovation to an existing building or property.

**REIT (real estate investment trust):** A publicly traded company that invests in real estate.

**rent control:** Tenant-protection laws that prevent landlords from increasing the rent.

**rent roll:** Total of current rent collected.

**rent stabilization:** Tenant-protection laws that dictate to the landlord how much to increase the rent each year.

# Glossary

revenue: Cash flowing in to you.

ROI: Return on investment.

rubber-stamp plans: Premade architectural blueprints that can be adjusted to any property with the same lot size.

scout: Also called a **bird dog**, a scout is the person who sniffs out the great deals and inside information real estate investors need. The designation is informal.

soft market: A market that features an oversupply of something and subsequent low demand for it.

turnaround: Restoring a poorly managed property to quality management; bringing a property that is not up to market rent, up to market rent.

violation: Any instance in which a property fails to meet local, state, or national regulations or laws.

walk-through inspection: Literally, a walk through the property for purchase just before the closing.

zoning: The regulations governing what kinds of buildings, sizes of buildings, and density of buildings (square footage compared with lot size) are allowed in a particular neighborhood. Zoning is determined and enforced at the town or city level.

# Index

# Index

# Index

# Index

# Index

# Index

# Index

# About the Authors

**Boaz Gilad** is President and founder of ORE International, a real estate development and management firm. Beginning with no capital of his own, Boaz has acquired ownership in real estate assets worldwide. Currently, he leads real estate seminars across the United States. Boaz lives in Brooklyn, New York and enjoys traveling with his wife and children—in pursuit of the next great real estate deal!

**Suzanne Gilad** leads seminars around the country on creating financial and time freedom. She is the founder of PaidToProofread.com and the author of GET PAID TO READ. Her voice can be heard on national commercials and films. Visit Sue at www.SuzanneGilad.com.